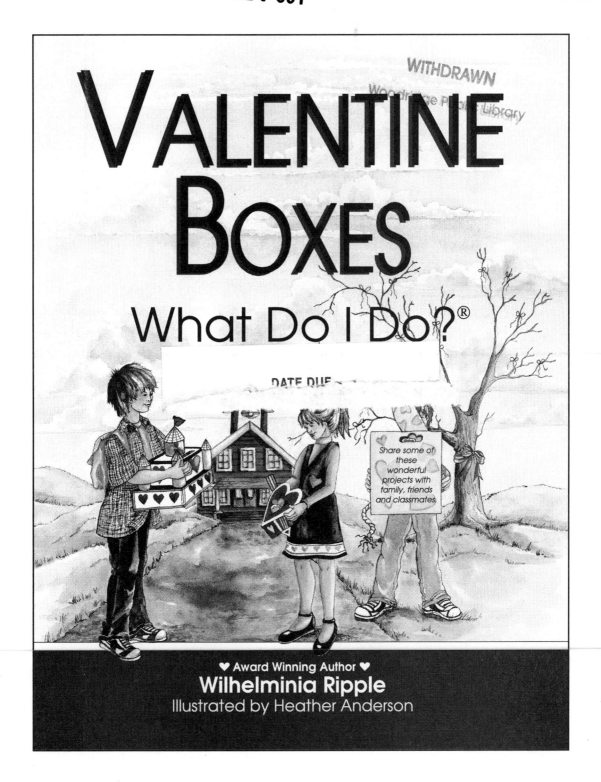

VALENTINE BOXES

What Do I Do?®

Share some of these wonderful projects with family, friends and classmates.

♥ Award Winning Author ♥
Wilhelminia Ripple
Illustrated by Heather Anderson

Valentine Boxes ... What Do I Do?®, author Wilhelminia Ripple

Oakbrook Publishing House
P.O. Box 2463
Littleton, Colorado 80161-2463
PHONE: (303) 738-1733 • FAX: (303) 797-1995
Or email us at: Oakbrook@whatdoidobooks.com
Website: **http://www.whatdoidobooks.com**

To order: 1-888-738-1733

Notice: The author and publisher have checked all directions and information very intently and put out this book together in good faith. However, the author and publisher assumes no responsibility for outcomes and disclaims all liabilities with using any information from this book

Publisher's Cataloging-in-Publication
(Provided by Quality Books, Inc.)

Ripple, Wilhelminia.
    Valentine boxes-- : what do I do? / Wilhelminia
Ripple ; illustrator, Heather Anderson ; editor,
Dianne Lorang. -- 1st ed.
    p. cm. -- (What do I do?)
    Includes index.
    LCCN: 99-75194
    ISBN: 0-9649939-3-7

    1. Valentine decorations. 2. Box craft
I. Title.

TT900. V34R57 1999   745.594'1
                              QBI99-1454

Printed and bound in the United States of America.

Printing 10 9 8 7 6 5 4 3 2 1

This Book is Happily Dedicated

**To creating memories
that will last a lifetime**
and
To my husband Mark
(who helps with all the challenges)
and
To my children Mark, Nick, and Michelle
(for being so patient and understanding)
and
To all who believe in me!

Acknowledgments

Special thanks to the schools, organizations, and companies who donated prizes for contest winners, and allowed us to hold our contests at their facility:

Mark Hopkins Elementary
Lewis Ames Elementary
Pine Lane Primary
Ralph Moody Elementary
Museum of Outdoor Arts

Southwest YMCA of Colorado
YMCA Jeffco Branch
Goodson Recreation Center
The Children's Museum of Denver
Discovery Zone

Special thanks to the following children who allowed me to share their winning Valentine boxes with you:

Laura Airey, Lance Allen, Vicki Anderson, Alyssa Arbuckle, Hannah Baird, Cindy Bastron, Becky Bathrick, Brady Bathrick, Andrea Betancourt, Dayne Bieghler, Lynn Bigelow, Alex Brown, Whitney Buckner, Christa Bueno, Dylan Buglewicz, Stevi Buglewicz, Schuyler Burks, Kevin Collins, Christopher Conrad, Mitchell Cowan, Casey D'Alanno, Robyn Delaney, Dominick Gamba, Gia Genitempo, Jason Hamblen, Kate Hanford, A. J. Haschke, Jonathan Henricks, Jaclyn Hodson, Steven Hodson, Alexzandria Holocher, Kevin Hurd, David Inbody, Evan Jaeger, Fritz Jaeger, Jenna James, Raeanne Johnson, Jacob Keller, Megan Knight, Jeff Kortman, Calvin Leas, Kjerstin Lewis, Jaime Liljegren, Samantha Lyle, Kelsie Maddock, Sabrina McCue, Phoebe McLaughlin, Thomas McNutt, Jordan Manley, Forrest Shawn-Lee Martin, Nicole Martens, Katie Markegard, Weston Markegard, Martin Milius, Britney Maynard, Ryan Miller, Sarah Miller, Carolyn Morris, Justin Moore, Becky Neuman, Dawn E. Noble, Judy Osborn, Samantha Post, Andy Putnam, Sydni Robson, Kathryn Rimmer, Michelle Ripple, Ashlie Rossel, Jennifer Ratterman, Risa Royal, Tyler Sale, Caroline Schafer, Erica Schumacher, Dennis Selph, Ian Setser, Tia Stanley, Wenzel Stoebe, Anna Taylor, Julia Terrell, Laura Thurlow, Moriah VanCleef, Nathan Walter, Taleen Woodard, Nick Wolf, Kirsten Wright and Diane Young.

Special thanks to the following who were patient in working with me:
Illustrator: Heather Anderson
Editor: Dianne Lorang of The Write Help
Cover Designer: Bobbi Shupe of E. P. Puffin & Company
Production Assistants: Lindsay Junkin, Pam Kortman, and Mark Ripple Jr.
Printer: Johnson Printing, Boulder, CO

And if I have forgotten you, "Thank You!"

About the Author

Wilhelminia "Willie" Ripple is the award-winning author of the *What Do I Do?*® series. She has sixteen years of experience in collecting and creating party ideas. Willie currently lives in Colorado with her husband Mark, and their three children.

To learn more about the What Do I Do? ® series, visit our web site at:

http://www.whatdoidobooks.com

Table of Contents

v

The Ark
Jaime Liljegren   49
Slot Machine
Tia Stanley   50
Sliding Valentines
Taleen Woodard   51
Spider–The Love Bug
Risa Royal   52
Valentines, Stars & Hearts, Oh My!
Wenzel Stoebe   53

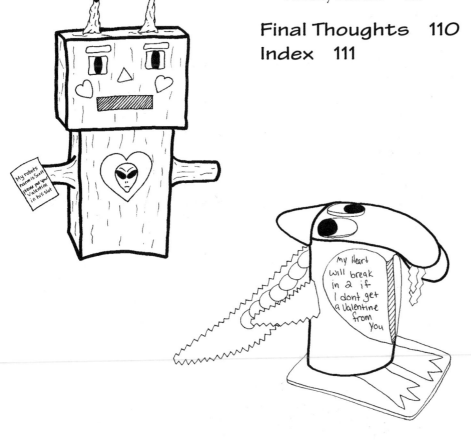

The Making of Valentine Boxes ... What Do I Do?(k)

The following Valentine Boxes where compiled from two years of contests, February 1998 and February 1999. The grades of the children reflect the year they were in the contest. The children were judged on elaboration, originality, and WOW!

Introduction
How To Use This Book

Valentine Boxes ... What Do I Do? ® gives you ideas for planning, and directions for making, great Valentine Boxes. Any age group can make Valentine Boxes but younger children typically take on this fun craft project for school, daycare, clubs, or just for the fun of it. This *What Do I Do?* ® book contains one-of-a-kind information about all aspects of making Valentine Boxes in eight chapters, including The What, Why & How of Valentine Boxes and seven chapters full of unique Valentine Boxes, each representing a theme: Cute, Unusual Card Slots, Creative Use of Candy, Recycled, Easy to Make, Jokes, Puns & Poems, and Bags & Envelopes.

After choosing a theme, take a few minutes to look at the award-winning boxes and their illustrations in that chapter. Decide which Valentine Box or Boxes you and your children like. If you are new to this fun craft project, there are basic supplies and directions in the How to Make a Valentine Box section. These directions will guide you through the process. If you have made Valentine Boxes before and need more of a challenge, try incorporating some of the difficult ideas from several types of boxes into one fantastic, unusual box. Also, important questions to ask yourself are listed in the Questions to Ask Yourself about Making Valentine Boxes section. Refer to it before, during, and after you make your box.

So remember to first choose a theme, the start of your successful Valentine Box, then go from there. Read the Helpful Hints and Chapter One. Then the fun begins! No more fussing, no more headaches. It couldn't be easier.

If you have a Valentine Box you would like us to consider putting in a future edition of *Valentine Boxes ... What Do I Do?* ®, send a photo, a list of supplies, and step-by-step directions to:

Oakbrook Publishing House
Valentine Box Entry
P.O. Box 2463
Littleton, CO 80161-2463

Key to Symbols
Used Throughout
this Book:

Knowledge Symbol
Theme-related educational facts to share with children.

Help Symbol
Adult help may be needed with gluing, cutting, or lengthy instructions.

Overnight Symbol
This box needs to dry overnight, so plan ahead.

Supply Symbol
Complete list of items needed for each Valentine Box, including tools.

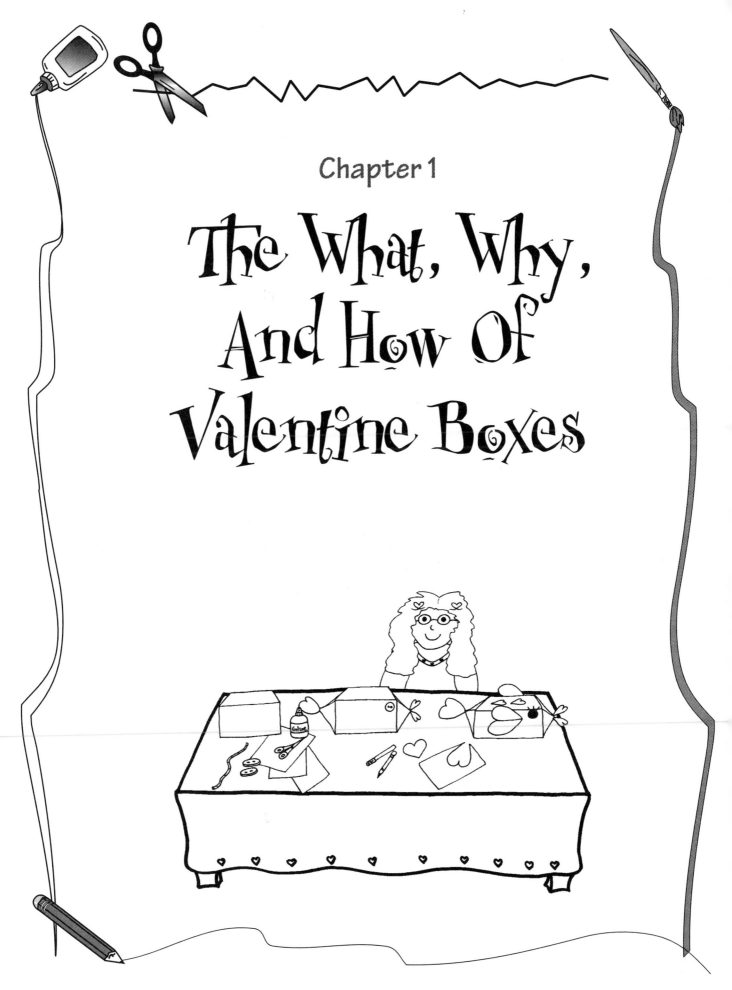

Chapter 1

The What, Why, And How Of Valentine Boxes

What Does Valentine's Day Mean To Us?

Parents, do you remember making Valentine Boxes? Tell us about it.

"My daughter Casey, a 6th grader, was out of town until the day before Valentine's Day. Before we left town we bought Valentine cards and candy to stuff into the envelopes, and she made a card for everyone in her class. On arriving back in town she learned they weren't exchanging Valentines this year—a big disappointment for MOM!"

—Judy Osborn, Parent

Describe the best box you ever made?

"The best box I ever made was an upside down "T" with two shoe boxes. On the inside there were a lot of interconnecting levers so each time you put a Valentine in the box a card would pop up that said Thank You. I enjoy making boxes because it is a fun hands on project."

—Jeff Kortman, Student

Do you enjoy making Valentine Boxes?

"Yes, because I like to create things."

—Kelsie Maddock, Student

February 14th is the special holiday when we honor St. Valentine. There are different stories about who he was and what he did. Today loved ones and friends trade tokens of affection, most often Valentine cards. Children's cards have cute designs and messages on them, and sell at most grocery and discount stores. It is a big deal for your children to pick out their own Valentines to share with their friends at school.

Most of the cards come in packages of 25 to 30, with one for the teacher. Some packages include candy to give with each card. Other Valentines fold into boxes or unique designs. *Caution:* These are cute and fun for kids to make, but they usually don't fit through the slots on other children's Valentine Boxes. Explain this to your child to help him or her decide whether to purchase these or not. Your child can always set them next to the boxes. Or your child can give this type to neighbors, family, and non-school friends, and then the traditional flat Valentine cards to classmates.

What Is A Valentine Box?

Just like we have mailboxes for our mail, children need something to collect all the Valentine cards they will receive. This is why we have Valentine Boxes. A child usually makes his or her own Valentine Box, which is *a container where other children deliver their Valentines to him or her*. Depending on the school (daycare or club), Valentine Boxes are made during school or at home and brought to school. Some schools/teachers opt for the children to make identical boxes or bags as a craft project, while others just ask that the children place their Valentines on each others' desks, or discourage or even ban Valentines altogether.

Why Make A Valentine Box?

We make Valentine Boxes to celebrate St. Valentine's Day and collect Valentine cards sent from friends, family, and teachers. Making a Valentine Box also helps kids express their identity as well as creativity. This is why children should be allowed to design their own boxes instead of making one from the teacher's pattern, not to mention it's more fun. As you go through this book, try to guess if a box was made by a boy or a girl and the grade of that child, and maybe something about his or her interests. (Don't peek in the column where the name and grade are listed.) Yes, in some cases there was an adult helper—see the How To Make A Valentine Box section (this chapter) for some tips in that area.

How Much Time Does It Take To Make A Valentine Box?

This question is especially helpful if your child and you are new to this whole process of making Valentine Boxes. Years ago, we were told to bring a shoebox to school, then given construction paper, crayons, scissors, and glue. That was it. We usually made our Valentine Boxes in an hour or less. Sometimes we had to follow exact directions on how to design and make our boxes. Other times we could create our own, but only by using the basic supplies. You can imagine the results—a lot of paper hearts glued on shoeboxes.

Now, the amount of time children put into making their Valentine Boxes depends on them. Do they like to create or just follow instructions? Do they work quickly? Is there something else they would rather be doing? Are they perfectionists, dreamers, or motivated? Are they young; do they need lots of breaks? The answers to these questions can help you determine what kind of time you will need.

Also, if a box needs to dry overnight, you'll see the overnight symbol next to the supply list. If you're in a hurry, most of the boxes in the Easy to Make chapter can be done in approximately one-half hour or less. On the average, your child can create one of the other boxes in two to three hours, once you have gathered the supplies. If you know your child takes a long time on projects, or likes to put his or her "all" into them, start at least a week early and have him or her do a little bit each day.

How To Make A Valentine Box

If this is your child's first time making a Valentine Box, have him or her go through the book to see the wide variety of boxes. Also see *Valentine School Parties … What Do I Do?®* for an additional 30 boxes. Your child may choose to make one of the boxes in our books, or looking may trigger an idea of his or her own. Remember, your child is forming an identity. Try not to guide him or her too much. If your child chooses a box in one of our books, your job is easy—you have a supply list and directions already there for you. *Caution:* An adult should supervise the making of some boxes.

Have your child read The Questions To Ask Yourself About Valentine Box Making section (at the end of this chapter). There are three parts: one to read before starting the box, one to read while making the box, and finally a part to read after finishing the Valentine Box. Here are some basic supplies and directions to help you through your first box. You'll find additional help when you read the Questions To Ask Yourself About Making Valentine Boxes section.

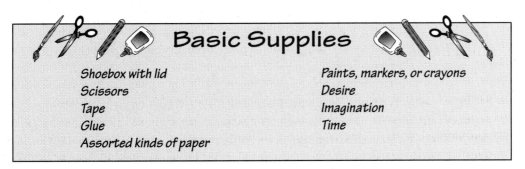

Basic Supplies

Shoebox with lid
Scissors
Tape
Glue
Assorted kinds of paper

Paints, markers, or crayons
Desire
Imagination
Time

Basic Directions

1. All boxes need an opening of some kind to deposit Valentine cards into. Throughout this book they're called slots. Keep in mind that a slot needs to be big enough for assorted size cards. Use scissors or a knife, with adult supervision.

2. You'll need to get your cards out. Will you shake them out of the slot, remove the lid, or rip open the box? It's your choice.

3. Each box needs covering. Some ways are to wrap the box like a present, paint it, or cover it with something such as aluminum foil, cloth, or construction paper—anything you want. You'll usually need tape or glue for this process.

4. Now for the rest of the fun—and by that, I mean the final touches on your creation:
    ❥ Glue or tape decorations and stuff to your box. (Stuff can be anything.)
    ❥ Cut shapes out of paper and other things, and glue them to your box.
    ❥ Draw on your box.
    ❥ Add things to your box, even other boxes, to make your box into something besides just another box. It's all up to you!

Do you, or your child, make your box yourself or as a family activity?

"When our son was little, he and I used to make the box as a family project. I would encourage him to do as much as possible to work on fine motor skills. But … it had to be fun! The best box we ever made was a woven heart-shaped basket (using two hearts and weaving like a placement) that we stapled a handle on."
　—Dawn E. Noble,
　　Parent

Parents, do you remember making Valentine Boxes? Tell us about it.

"Yes, it was always so exciting. I wanted the attention of the boys and I wanted to make the slot for the envelopes big enough for candy. I used to like to use pink and red crepe paper, glitter, Valentine candy hearts, stickers, and red hots. I would keep my box around for weeks."
　—Vicki Anderson,
　　Parent

Supplies You May Never Have Thought Of Using To Make Your Valentine Box ...

Hat box	Candy
Dishwasher detergent box	Charms
Laundry detergent box	Compass
Shoe/boot box	Cookie cutters
Construction paper	Cupcake/muffin cups
Con-Tact® paper	Embroidery thread/floss
Crepe paper	Fabric
Red foil	Flowers
Stickers	Lace
Old jewelry	Magazines
Yarn	Greeting cards
Newspaper	Christmas ornaments
Tissue paper	Perfume samples
Wrapping paper	Pipe cleaners
Paper doilies	Photographs of yourself, friends, family,
Paper clips	and places
Crayons	Satin ribbon
Markers	Jewels
Paints	Valentine cards
Pencils	Tempera paints
Pens	Paintbrushes
Double-stick tape	Poems
Tape	Curling ribbon
Glitter	Toothpicks
Glue	Stamps
Glue stick	Stamp pad
Paste	Stickers
Ruler	String
Scissors	Yarn
Beads	

Where to Find Supplies

Art supply stores	Hardware stores
Craft stores	Home-improvement stores
Fabric stores	Office supply stores
Grocery stores	Discount stores

And don't forget about Garage Sales and your own discards ...

Questions To Ask Yourself About Making Valentine Boxes

Ask these questions before making your box:

❧ Do I have to carry the box to and from school (daycare or club)?

❧ What supplies do I already have at home? What do I have to buy?

❧ Where will the card slot go to deposit Valentines? How will I get the cards out of the box?

❧ When do I have to start the box? How much time do I need? Should I break the project up into little steps (do some each day)?

❧ When does the box need to be at school (daycare or club)?

Ask these questions while making your box:

❧ Do I need help with making my box? What kind and how much help?

❧ If someone gives me a large Valentine or one stuffed with candy, will it go through my slot?

❧ I'm missing a supply item—what can I substitute for it?

❧ Can I make the box smaller, taller, fatter, thinner, a different color? Can I animate it, take away something, add something—what?

❧ I'm having fun and I want to keep working on my box *but* did I finish all my homework and chores?

Ask these questions after your box is made:

❧ Did I remember everything? Can I do something else?

❧ Did I take a picture of my box so I'll remember it forever?

❧ Do I want to save this box? If I'm going to throw it away, can I save pieces from it?

❧ What did I learn? What did I like and dislike about making my box?

❧ Did I have fun?

Describe the best box you or your child ever made?

"One year, my son made his Valentine Box out of a Victoria's Secret box. The box was bright pink with gold outlined hearts on it. All he had to do was cut a slot for his cards to go in. It was so easy, and it looked so good."
—Lynn Bigelow, Parent

Parents, do you remember making Valentine Boxes? Tell us about it.

"I remember helping my children with their boxes. Their excitement brought back memories of my own anticipation. Here's a description of the best box my son, a 5th grader, made. It was a tank Valentine Box. We covered a large box bottom in white paper, turned it upside down and taped a smaller box, also covered, on top and added a covered toilet paper tube. He decorated the box with hearts all over. Then he put his remote control car under it, and he had a moving Valentine Box! The smaller box on top had the slot and held the Valentines. It was the hit of the 5th grade Valentine party."
—Diane Young, Parent

Helpful Hints For Valentine Boxes

To decide what type of Valentine Box to make, choose a theme to give you direction.

Do not forget to cut a slot to deposit Valentines, as well as devise a way to get your cards out.

There is no idea too wild!

Bags and envelopes can also be turned into some great Valentine Boxes.

For very young children, use safety scissors with a rounded tip.

A slot can always be in a unique shape, such as an arrow.

Throughout the year, save all different kinds of boxes and containers, such as shoeboxes, boot boxes, laundry detergent boxes, cereal boxes, tissue boxes, oatmeal containers, and milk bottles. Large ones work best.

To prevent injury, adults should cut slots in the Valentine boxes for young children. A knife might work better than the scissors in each supply list.

Also have adult supervision for glue guns, X-acto® knives, or other sharp or potentially dangerous tools.

Double-backed tape or Velcro® can be used to hold items on your Valentine Box.

Helpful Hints For Valentine Boxes

Moving eyes are sometimes called "wiggly" eyes or "googly" eyes.

When you need to paint, let the paint dry thoroughly before adding an additional coat.

When personalizing a box with another word after your name, add an "s" and apostrophe to your name, such as "Jill's Valentine Box."

Take pictures and/or videos so you'll have lasting memories.

Spell a Valentine word (such as LOVE) with candy on top of your box. Large heart chewy candies work well.

A paper fastener is also called a "brad" and a Popsicle® stick is the same thing as a craft stick. And, cellophane wrap can be substituted with plastic wrap.

There are lots of glues to choose from: glue guns, school glue, glue sticks, paste, etc. When using a glue gun, hold the item in place for a few seconds. The glue dries quickly.

In some cases, we list the quantity of supplies needed, but sometimes we don't. So read the directions before assembling your supplies and you'll be able to determine the amount you'll need.

If you put a decoration on the side of a box with a lid, be sure to put the decoration above or below the lid. You can also cut a decoration (such as a sticker) in half, and put one half on the lid and the other on the side, matching the halves up, of course.

HAVE FUN!

Chapter 2
Cute Boxes

by
Anna Taylor

Grade 4

Curious Anna

Supplies

Shoebox with lid
Sparkling wrapping paper
Tape
Scissors
Monkey stuffed animal
Scrap of fabric
Pacifier

Glue
Conversation candy hearts
Small jewelry box with lid
Pink construction paper
Red glitter pen
Small Valentine and envelope

Directions

1. Wrap the shoebox, top and bottom separately, with the sparkling wrapping paper. Tape to secure.

2. Cut a slot in the shoebox lid to deposit the Valentines.

3. Put a "diaper" on the monkey using the scrap of fabric.

4. Insert the pacifier into the monkey's mouth.

5. Glue the monkey to the top of the shoebox lid, to the left of the slot.

6. Glue the conversation hearts around the slot and near the monkey.

7. Wrap the entire small jewelry box with the sparkling wrapping paper. Tape to secure.

8. Cut a slit in the small box using your scissors. (This is only for "show" rather than use.)

9. Glue the jewelry box to the top right corner of the shoebox lid.

10. Cut out two medium hearts from the pink construction paper.

11. Use the red glitter pen to write "Happy Valentine's Day" on each heart.

12. Glue one heart onto the monkey's hand.

13. Glue the other heart sticking up from the back edge of the small jewelry box with the words facing forward.

14. Cut out eight tiny hearts from the pink construction paper and glue them around the slit of the small jewelry box.

15. Glue the small Valentine and envelope separately to the top of the shoebox lid in front of the jewelry box.

Optional: If the monkey's mouth is not "open," attach the pacifier with yarn or string and hang it from the monkey's neck, or cut the nipple off the pacifier and glue the pacifier onto the monkey's mouth.

Three-Tier Valentine Box

Supplies

Pencil
Scissors
Small square box with top
Medium square box with top
Large square box with top

Red cellophane wrap
Tape
Gold sequins
Antique gold heart-shaped buttons
Gold heart doilies

Optional: Boxes can also be rectangular but should all be the same shape.

by
Megan Knight

Grade 5

Directions

1. Draw a medium heart shape on the center of each box top. Be sure the hearts are the same size and wider than Valentines.

2. Use the scissors to cut out each heart.

3. Wrap each box with the red cellophane, leaving the heart-shaped holes open. Tape to secure.

4. Match up the heart-shaped holes and glue all three boxes together, smallest on top, medium in the middle, and largest on the bottom.

5. Randomly glue gold sequins, gold heart-shaped buttons, and gold heart doilies to all the boxes.

6. Valentines will be deposited into the heart-shape hole in the smallest box and drop down to the largest box. To retrieve them, simply shake them out.

Can you think of any words that rhyme with the word cute? Here's some to get you started: loot, boot, flute, mute, hoot, suit, root, fruit, and toot.

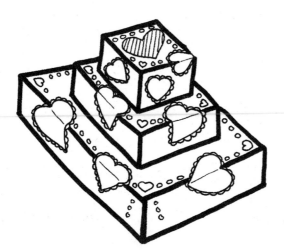

Cute Boxes

by
Carolyn Morris
Grade 3

Love Bunny Valentine Basket

Supplies

Plastic grocery bag
Six rubber bands
Styrofoam® ball
Round cardboard container with lid
Gray felt
Glue gun
Pencil
Scissors
Pink felt

Poster board
White felt
Red felt
Fishing line
Moving eyes
Small Valentine balloon on stick
Small red basket
Curling ribbon (any color)
32 inches Valentine's Day ribbon

Directions

1. Squish the plastic grocery bag into a small ball and use rubber bands to attach it to the Styrofoam® ball (head) to shape the front of the rabbit's face.

2. Wrap the round cardboard container and lid (body) and the Styrofoam® ball (head) with gray felt. Glue to secure.

3. Use a pencil to poke a hole into the lid of the round container (body). Then poke a hole into the Styrofoam® ball (head), leaving the pencil in the hole.

4. Slide the pencil with the head attached into the hole in the body. Glue to secure.

5. Cut one pair of rabbit ears out of gray felt and another pair out of pink felt.

6. Glue one pink felt ear to the underside of one gray felt ear to make one ear. Repeat this step for the second ear.

7. Glue one ear on each side of the top of the head, pink side down.

8. Cut a pair of rabbit arms and a pair of rabbit feet from the poster board.

9. Cut two pieces of white felt to fit each arm and foot (eight total). Glue one piece on each side of each arm and foot.

10. Cut three 1½-inch hearts from the red felt and six 1-inch hearts from the pink felt.

11. Glue one red heart to each foot for the heels. Glue three pink hearts to each foot for the toes.

12. Glue the remaining red heart to the face for the bunny's nose.

Cute Boxes

Love Bunny Valentine Basket (cont.)

by
Carolyn Morris

Grade 3

13. Cut two thin strips of pink felt and glue onto the face to form a mouth. Glue on whiskers made from fishing line.

14. Glue moving eyes to the face just above the nose.

15. Glue the arms to the back of the body just below the head.

16. Glue the legs flat against the front of the body, bottoms facing forward.

17. Glue the Valentine balloon to one hand and the basket to the other hand. Valentines are to be deposited in the basket.

18. Curl the curling ribbon with the scissors and glue it to the top of the bunny's head for hair.

19. Cut the Valentine's Day ribbon into a 12-inch and a 20-inch piece.

20. Tie the 20-inch piece of Valentine ribbon around the bunny's neck.

21. Make a bow from the 12-inch piece of Valentine ribbon and attach to the hair.

Cute Boxes

23

by
Steven Hodson

Grade 1

Basketball Player

 Supplies

Red spray paint
Shoebox with lid
Scissors
Glue gun
Paper towel tube
7 x 12-inch piece gold wrapping paper

White yarn
Markers or crayons
White poster board
Craft stick
Black permanent marker

Directions

1. Thoroughly spray paint the shoebox and lid separately with red paint.

2. After the shoebox is dry, cut a slot in the lid to deposit Valentines.

3. Cover the paper towel tube with the gold wrapping paper. Glue to secure.

4. Cut off ½-inch from the paper towel tube and save for a basketball hoop.

5. Stand the paper towel tube (basketball pole) on top of the shoebox lid, either side of the slot, and glue in place.

6. Glue the basketball hoop to the outside of the basketball pole tube near the top and facing towards the slot in the shoebox lid.

7. "Weave" a net for the basketball hoop using the white yarn. Secure with glue.

8. Draw and color a basketball player on the poster board.

9. Cut out the player, and glue the craft stick onto his back, leaving approximately an inch of stick past his feet.

10. Make a small slit in the top of the box opposite the basketball pole and insert the basketball player. Glue if needed.

11. With the permanent marker, write "I love basketball" on a strip of poster board and glue onto the top of the box in front of the slot.

Optional: Add your favorite basketball team's name and logo to the box.

Funny Face Valentine Container

Supplies

by
Stevi Buglewicz

Grade 4

Round cardboard container with lid
Pink punch ball balloon (found at any
   discount or party store)
Scissors
Glue
1-inch red pom-poms
¼-inch white pom-poms

Long thin feathers (found in craft
   stores)
Two 15mm moving eyes
Feather boa
Hair clip
Novelty or old glasses
Red glitter

Directions

1. Put the lid on the container.
2. Pull the punch ball balloon over the lid of the container.
3. Carefully cut a large mouth-shape opening in the lid of the container
4. Glue red pom-poms around the mouth opening to form lips.
5. Glue white pom-poms to the lips for teeth.
6. Glue long thin feathers (top eyelashes) onto the face where you will be positioning the eyes.
7. Cut some feathers for bottom eyelashes and glue just below the top ones.
8. Glue the moving eyes onto the eyelashes.
9. Glue red glitter to the cheek area.
10. Glue the feather boa around the container to form hair.
11. Lay the container on its side and attach the hair clip to the feather boa.
12. Place glasses on the "face." Glue if needed.

Cute Boxes

by

Jordan Manley

Grade 1

Birdhouse Valentine Card Box

  ## Supplies

Pencil
20 x 22-inch foam board or
   cardboard
X-acto® knife
Scissors
Glue gun
3 inches ⁵/₁₆" wooden dowel

60 inches 2" red crepe paper
60 inches 2" pink crepe paper
Red construction paper
Conversation candy hearts
Large stuffed bird
Six small stuffed birds
Small red and pink plastic beads

Directions

1. Trace the following pattern pieces onto the foam board or cardboard and cut out: two roofs (pattern piece #1), two sides (pattern piece #2), one bottom (pattern piece #3), one front (pattern piece #4), and one back (pattern piece #5).

2. Clip the front and back as shown in pattern pieces #4 and #5. Save these clipped pieces for later. Cut a heart-shape hole in the front as shown in the pattern, with the X-acto® knife.

3. Glue the front and back clipped corners down to the bottom of the birdhouse, the back flush with the rear edge and the front flush with the front edge. They should be 9 inches apart.

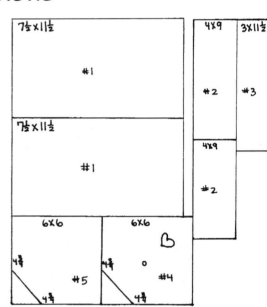

4. Glue the two sides to the lower edges of the front and back to form the bottom sides of the birdhouse.

5. Cut a slot in one piece of the roof to deposit Valentines. Fit the two roof pieces onto the remaining edges of the front and back, two long sides together at the peak. Glue together at the peak without securing to the birdhouse since the roof will be removed to take out Valentines.

6. Place the two triangular remnants clipped from the front and back in step #2 on the interior "V" of the roof to reinforce it, one ¼″ from each end. Both triangles must fit inside the birdhouse.

Cute Boxes

Birdhouse Valentine Card Box *(cont.)*

by
Jordan Manley
Grade 1

7. Glue the dowel to the front of the birdhouse as shown in pattern piece #4.

8. Cut both the red and pink crepe paper into 11½-inch strips for the roof shingles. You will have five strips of each color.

9. Alternating red and pink, glue the crepe paper onto the roof from front to back, overlapping slightly, to form shingles.

10. Cut, fold, and glue 1-inch strips of red construction paper to cover up the edges of the birdhouse, not the roof.

11. Glue conversation hearts around the heart "bird hole" on the front.

12. Glue the large bird to the wooden dowel.

13. Glue five small birds to the roof and one in the heart "bird hole."

14. Glue the beads around the roofline.

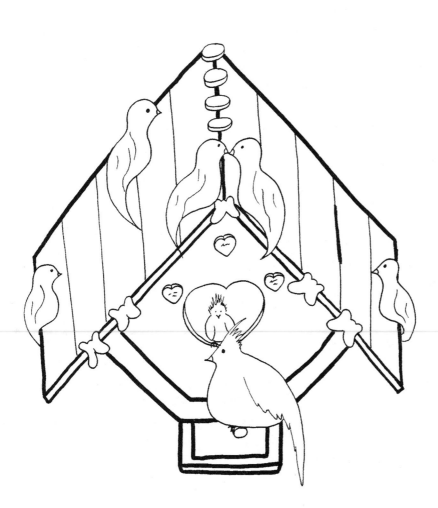

Cute Boxes

by
Evan Jaeger

Grade 5

Valentine House

Supplies

Coffee can with lid
Pink construction paper
Glue
Gold pipe cleaner
Three green pipe cleaners

Scissors
Corrugated cardboard
Mini fence (found at craft stores)
Three red pipe cleaners

Directions

1. Cover the coffee can with the pink construction paper. Glue to secure. Do not cover the lid.

2. Form a door from the gold pipe cleaner and glue it onto the bottom edge of the coffee can.

3. Shape each green pipe cleaner to form flower stems and leaves and set aside.

4. Cut three hearts out of the corrugated cardboard for flowers.

5. Poke one pipe cleaner flower stem through one heart flower, then poke it back through as if sewing on a button. Twist to secure on the back side of the flower. Repeat this process to make the other two flowers.

6. Glue the flowers 2 inches above the bottom edge of the coffee can, a couple of inches away from each other.

7. Glue the fence all the way around the bottom edge of the coffee can over the flower stems.

8. Shape two of the red pipe cleaners into windows, and glue them above the door.

10. Make a small hole in the coffee can lid and stick the end of the third red pipe cleaner inside the hole. Shape the pipe cleaner into a heart and twist to secure.

11. Cut a slot in the lid to deposit Valentines.

Home Sweet Home

by
Kathryn Rimmer

Grade 5

Supplies

Shoebox with lid
Red wrapping paper
Tape
Scissors
Two white pieces poster boards
Glue

Three cartoon character Valentines
Red permanent marker
Cardboard
Conversation candy hearts
Dollhouse mailbox

Directions

1. Cover the shoebox, lid attached, with red wrapping paper. Tape to secure.

2. Cut a large opening in the box on one long narrow side.

3. Fold one piece of poster board in half lengthwise to form the roof. *Note:* The other piece will be used for the yard plus smaller items.

4. Cut a slot on one side of the roof to deposit the Valentines.

5. Glue the roof on top of the box making sure the slot fits over the large opening in the box.

6. Glue two of the Valentines onto the opposite side of the box for windows. Glue thin strips of poster board across the Valentines for windowpanes.

7. Cut out a piece of poster board twice the size of the remaining Valentine. Fold the poster board in half and glue the Valentine to the inside. Glue the poster board onto the front of the house for a door, so the Valentine can be seen when the door is open.

8. Draw a heart doorknob and heart window with the red permanent marker on the outside of the door. Write "Happy Valentine's Day" on the front side of the roof.

9. Lay the second piece of poster board over the cardboard and glue to secure.

10. Glue the house to the top of the covered cardboard, leaving plenty of room for a front yard.

11. Use the conversation candy hearts to form a sidewalk from the door to the front of the yard. Glue to secure.

12. Glue the mailbox in the front yard.

13. Cut miniature Valentines from poster board.

14. Draw a heart on each with the red permanent marker. Place a few in the mailbox and glue some to the ground around the mailbox.

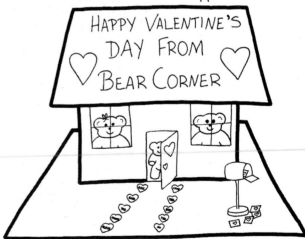

Cute Boxes

by

Samantha Lyle

Grade K

Memories

Supplies

Large gift box
Plain white paper
Tape
Scissors
Glue

Photographs of school, vacations,
friends, and family
Red construction paper
Conversation candy hearts

Directions

1. Wrap the entire box with plain white paper. Tape to secure.
2. Cut a slot in the top of the box to deposit the Valentines.
3. Randomly glue the photographs onto the box. Trim them if needed.
4. Cut out several hearts, different sizes and shapes, from the red construction paper and randomly glue onto the box.
5. Glue conversation hearts and paper hearts onto the box.

Cute Boxes

Teddy Bear's Box

Supplies

by
Jenna James
Grade 4

Large shoebox with lid
Shiny red paper (found in art stores)
Tape
Glue
Gold heart-shaped doily
Scissors

Valentine heart stickers (six small,
    six medium, one large gold)
Small teddy bear figurine
Silk flowers
60 inches ⅛" white ribbon

Directions

1. Wrap the shoebox, top and bottom separately, with the shiny red paper. Tape to secure.

2. Glue the doily onto the shoebox lid.

3. Cut a slot through the doily and the lid to deposit Valentines.

4. Decorate the shoebox lid with small heart stickers.

5. Glue the teddy bear figurine to any corner on the lid.

6. Glue the silk flower to the corner opposite the bear.

7. Cut the ribbon into six 10-inch pieces.

8. Tie each ribbon into a bow and glue to the sides of the box, placing two bows on each long side and one bow on each short side.

9. Stick a medium heart sticker in the center of each bow.

10. Stick the large gold heart sticker to the top of the box in the corner next to the bear.

Cute Boxes

by
Laura Thurlow

Grade 5

Frog Box

Supplies

Tape
Large box with flaps
Green construction paper
Stapler
Tacky glue
Scissors

Pinking shears
White construction paper
Black permanent marker
Red construction paper
White doily

Directions

1. Tape up the large box so the flaps are closed.

2. Cover the box with green construction paper. Staple or glue to secure.

3. Stand the box on its short side.

4. Cut a mouth slot near the top of the box to deposit the Valentines.

5. Use the pinking shears to cut a large heart from the green construction paper for the face.

6. Cut two 2-inch eyes out of the white construction paper and glue onto the face.

7. Using the black permanent marker, color in the pupil of each eye and draw a nose.

8. Cut two small hearts from the red construction paper and glue to the face for cheeks.

9. Glue the face to the front top of the box. Cut a mouth slot through the paper exactly where it is on the box.

10. Glue a doily to the front of the box under the mouth.

11. Cut four 2-inch strips of green construction paper for the legs and arms. Cut the ends into hands and feet.

12. Glue the arms to the sides of the box, bend them and glue the hands to the doily.

13. Glue the legs to the bottom of the box.

Bead-It

Supplies

Shoebox with lid
White wrapping paper
Tape
Scissors
Beads (assorted colors)

Glue
Red construction paper
18 inches ⅛" white ribbon
Curling ribbon (assorted colors)
Red glitter

by
Brady Bathrick
Grade 1
with a variation from Becky Bathrick
Grade 4

Directions

1. Wrap the shoebox, top and bottom separately, with the white wrapping paper. Tape to secure.
2. Cut a slot in the shoebox lid to deposit the Valentines.
3. Using the beads, spell out your name and glue it to the side of the shoebox.
4. Form a heart shape from the beads on the shoebox lid, then glue them in place.
5. Cut three hearts from the red construction paper. Glue two to the shoebox lid and one on the side of the box near your beaded name.
6. Cut the ribbon into three 6-inch pieces. Tie into bows and glue one onto each red heart.
7. Using the beads, form designs on the top of the box and glue them in place.
8. Curl some curling ribbon with the scissors and glue to three corners of the shoebox.
9. Glue glitter to the shoebox lid inside the beaded heart.

Variation: Spell your name out with red ⅛" ribbon rather than beads and wrap the shoebox and lid as one piece.

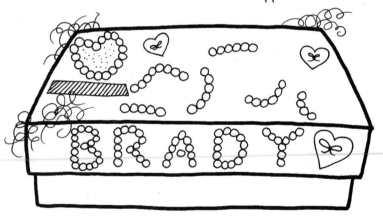

Cute Boxes

33

by
Ashlie Rossel

Grade 2

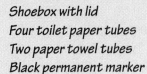

Giraffe

Supplies

Shoebox with lid
Four toilet paper tubes
Two paper towel tubes
Black permanent marker

Two moving eyes
Felt (assorted colors)
Yellow fabric
Glue gun

Directions

1. Cover the entire shoebox, four toilet paper tubes, and two paper towel tubes with the yellow fabric. Glue to secure.

2. Cut a slot in the shoebox lid to deposit Valentines

3. Cut the paper towel tube in half and squeeze it into the other paper towel tube to make the giraffe's head and neck. Glue to secure

4. Cut a hole in the shoebox lid big enough to insert the giraffe's neck. Glue to secure.

5. Fray some yellow fabric for the giraffe's mane and tail. Glue the mane on the neck and head, and the tail on the opposite end of the shoebox lid.

6. Glue the moving eyes onto the head, one on each side.

7. Cut out heart shapes from the felt, and glue to the front of the giraffe's neck.

8. Glue the toilet paper tubes upright to the bottom of the shoebox for legs.

9. Use the black permanent marker to draw spots on the giraffe.

Cute Boxes

34

Name Box

Supplies

Shoebox with lid
White wrapping paper
Glue

Scissors
Confetti
Construction paper (assorted colors)

by
**Christopher
Conrad**

Grade 1

Directions

1. Cover the shoebox and lid together with the white wrapping paper and glue to secure.

2. Cut a slot in shoebox lid to deposit and retrieve the Valentines.

3. Glue confetti to the shoebox lid.

4. Cut out the letters of your name from construction paper.

5. Spell out your name and glue it around the front, and right side of the shoebox.

6. Cut out assorted size hearts from the construction paper and glue to the backside of the box, overlapping one another.

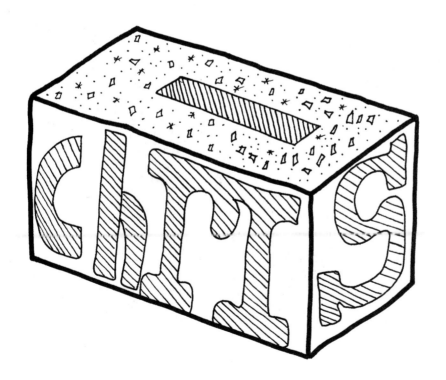

Cute Boxes

by
Christa Bueno
Grade 1

Valentine Person

Supplies

Empty oatmeal container with lid
Red tissue paper
Glue
Pencil
Ruler
Construction paper (assorted colors)
Scissors

Pinking shears
Two large heart beads
Red glitter
Red doily
Tape
Curling ribbon (assorted colors)

Directions

1. Set the oatmeal lid aside. Wrap the container with the red tissue paper and glue to secure. Tuck the excess paper into the open top of the oatmeal container to hide it.

2. Using the pencil, trace the ruler onto the construction paper four times. Cut out the ruler shapes, and then fold them back and forth like an accordion for the arms and legs. Set aside.

3. Using the pinking shears, cut out three hearts—two medium ones for the feet and one larger one for the hands to hold.

4. Glue a medium heart to each leg, and then glue the legs to the bottom of the container.

5. Glue the arms to the side of the container, and then bring them both to the front. Glue the larger heart on top of them to hold them in place.

6. Glue the beads on the front of the canister for the eyes.

7. Cut out glasses from construction paper and glue over the bead eyes.

8. Cut a mouth from construction paper and glue onto the face. Add glue then glitter for sparkly lips.

9. Glue the red doily on the lid of the container, then trim to fit.

10. Tape pieces of curling ribbon to the inside of the lid for hair. Curl the ribbon with the scissors.

11. Cut a slot in the lid to deposit Valentines.

Cute Boxes

 # Valentine Monkey

by
Justin Moore

Grade 1

Supplies

Half gallon empty milk carton
Red construction paper
Glue gun
Scissors
Pink construction paper
White construction paper

Black construction paper
One black pom-pom
Green construction paper
Red star stickers
One red pom-pom

Directions

1. Cover the milk carton with red construction paper and glue to secure.

2. Cut out a large monkey face shape from red construction paper and a smaller face from pink construction paper.

3. Glue the pink face to the red face.

4. Cut two small circles out of white construction paper for eyes. Glue to the face.

5. Cut two tiny circles out of black construction paper for the pupils. Glue to the eyes.

6. Glue the black pom-pom to the face for the nose.

7. Cut a large hole in one side of the top of the milk carton to deposit Valentines.

8. Glue the face over the hole in the milk carton.

9. Cut a smiling mouth in the face over the hole in the milk carton.

10. Cut two hands and two feet out of red construction paper. Glue the hands to the sides and the feet to the bottom of the milk carton.

11. Cut out hearts from pink construction paper and glue all around the carton.

12. Make a cone hat from green construction paper. Glue to the top of the monkey's head.

13. Cut out the letter "V" (for Valentine) from pink construction paper. Glue to the hat.

14. Attach red star stickers to the hat.

15. Glue the red pom-pom to the tip of the monkey's hat.

Cute Boxes

Chapter 3

Unusual Card Slot Boxes

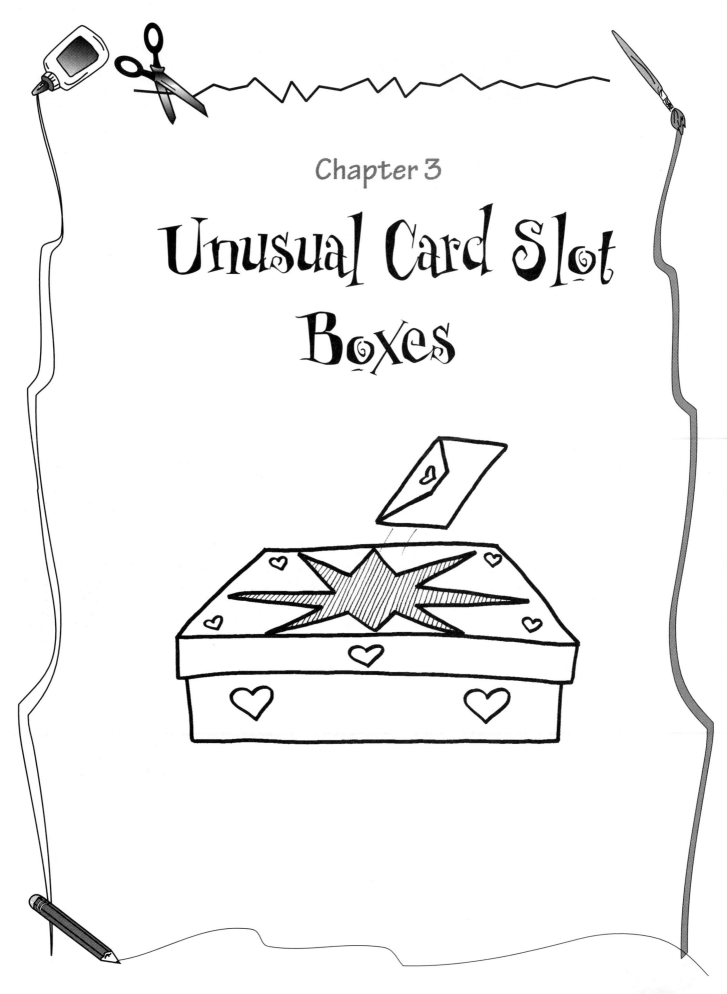

by
Sarah Miller
Grade 5

There is more than one way to use playing cards. You can join a club on the Internet that collects playing cards. These clubs have meetings where you can trade playing cards with others. Check them out.

Unusual Card Slot Boxes

Down the Chute

Supplies

Purple spray paint
Shoebox with lid
Glue gun
Pink construction paper
Scissors
Two pieces 6 x 10-inch white poster
    board

Paper hole puncher
Six 10-inch pieces curling ribbon
    (different colors)
Assorted Valentine candy
Valentine stickers

Directions

1. Spray paint the shoebox and lid purple and let dry.
2. Glue the pink construction paper onto the center top of the lid.
3. Cut a slot 6 inches long in the lid of the shoebox to deposit the Valentines.
4. Put the two pieces of poster board together, and then punch three holes in each long side about 4 inches apart and ½-inch from the edges.
5. Thread a piece of curling ribbon through each hole, tie tightly, and curl the ends with the scissors.
6. Push the poster board through the 6-inch slot in the shoebox lid. Pull the pieces of poster board slightly apart so Valentines can be deposited through this "chute."
7. Glue candy on the sides of the shoebox and to the top of the lid.
8. Decorate the chute with Valentine stickers.

The Broken Heart

  ## Supplies

by
Andy Putnam
Grade 5

Shoebox with lid
White, blue, pink, and red
    construction paper
Tape

Scissors
Glue
Two small red beads

Directions

1. Wrap the shoebox, top and bottom separately, with white paper. Tape to secure.
2. Cut a ½ x 3-inch slot in the middle of the shoebox lid.
3. Cut a piece of blue construction paper in half, and then fold it to fit snugly into the slot, leaving it "hollow" to deposit Valentines through. Only push it far enough in the slot to secure with glue.
4. Cut out the front of this "chute" so it "slants" forward.
5. Cut out a 4-inch pink heart and cut a jagged line through the middle of it.
6. With the red construction paper, cut out a second heart twice the size of the pink heart. Cut a slot in the center of the large red heart that will fit around the chute.
7. Glue the very outer edges of the pink heart to the red heart.
8. Glue a red bead on each half of the pink heart for door handles to let you open the heart and slide the Valentines down the chute.
9. Carefully glue the combined hearts to the chute so that the slot of the red heart fits over the chute opening.
10. Using the leftover construction paper, cut out hearts of various sizes. Glue to the broken heart chute and box for decoration.

Unusual Card Slot Boxes

by
Hannah Baird

Grade K

Valentine-Eating Monster

  ## Supplies

Pencil	Scissors
Black foam core board	½" ribbon
X-acto® knife	Velcro® (with adhesive backing)
Glue gun	Neon orange paper
Markers, crayons, and/or paint	Black permanent marker
White construction paper	

Directions

1. With the pencil, have an adult help design a box and lid on black foam core board. Use the X-acto® knife to cut out the box parts.

2. Using the glue gun, glue the box and lid pieces together.

3. Using the markers and crayons on a piece of white construction paper, draw and color a monster head (see illustration) with a large mouth in the center of the head. Cut the shape and mouth out.

4. Cut out another piece of paper the exact same size as the monster head and color it to represent the bow of the "package."

5. Use an X-acto® knife to cut an opening in the box lid to match the shape of the monster mouth you drew. This will be to deposit Valentines.

6. With a pencil, trace the monster head onto black foam core board. Using an X-acto® knife, carefully cut out the head shape and mouth opening.

7. Glue the monster head onto the foam core board and carefully bend it in half so the monster head is on the inside. This breaks the foam core in half but not the paper, giving the mouth a hinge.

Valentine-Eating Monster *(cont.)*

by
Hannah Baird
Grade K

8. Flatten out the monster head and glue the bow (except the area by the mouth, which you will secure in step #9) on the other side of it. Bend the head back as it was and trim out the "monster mouth" from the bow.

9. Hook the monster head to the box lid by making tabs from ribbon and gluing them on the bow side (the outside) near the break and onto the box lid. Finish gluing the bow to the monster head.

10. Cut a piece of ribbon long enough to go from the center front of the monster head to the center back. Cut a short piece of Velcro®. Glue one end of the ribbon to one piece of the Velcro® and the other end of the ribbon (with no Velcro®) to the front center of the bow. Glue the other piece of the Velcro® to the center back of the bow. Close the bow, attaching the Velcro® pieces. It will be a surprise when your friends open up the bow and see they deposit their Valentines through the monster mouth.

11. Cut a nametag from the foam core board. Trace the nametag onto the neon orange paper and cut out. Glue the paper and foam core board nametags together. Using a black permanent marker, write "Open my bow and feed me Valentines" on the neon paper.

12. Use the scissors to carefully punch a hole in the nametag. Slide a piece of ribbon through the hole and the monster mouth on the bow and tie.

13. Decorate the box and lid to look like a present using ribbon and hearts cut from white construction paper, then colored.

Unusual Card Slot Boxes

by
Ian Setser

Grade 3

Valentine Slide Box

  ## Supplies

Shoebox with lid
White tissue paper
Scissors
Tape
Medium weight cardboard

Three craft sticks
Glue
Red construction paper
Silver glitter pen

Directions

1. Wrap the shoebox, top and bottom separately, with the white tissue paper. Tape to secure.

2. Cut a square opening in one corner of the top of the lid, big enough to deposit Valentines.

3. Cut and fold the medium weight cardboard to form the "slide." Wrap it with white tissue paper and glue to secure.

4. Glue one craft stick to each side of the slide to form two support poles.

5. Cut six heart shapes from the red construction paper and glue to all sides of the box.

6. Using a glitter pen, write "Happy Valentine's" on the top of the lid.

7. Poke two small slits into the lid, opposite the square opening, to stick the slide's support poles.

8. Glue the third craft stick between the two support poles.

The Valentine Boat

by
Alex Brown

Grade 2

Supplies

Shoebox with lid
White construction paper
Tape
Scissors
Red poster board
Stapler
Glue

Toothpick
Small heart stickers
Fish stickers
Large heart stickers
Crayons
Pipe cleaner
Yarn

Directions

1. Wrap the shoebox, top and bottom separately, with the construction paper. Tape to secure.

2. Cut a rectangular shape from the poster board for the boat's smokestack. Shape it into a cylinder, then staple to secure. *Note:* Make sure the cylinder is big enough around for Valentines to pass through it.

3. Cut two identical long rectangular boat shapes from poster board. Lay one on top of the other and staple together at both ends. Open up the "boat" and slide it over the smokestack.

4. Cut a slot in the center of the shoebox lid to deposit the Valentines. Place the center of the boat over the slot.

5. Glue both the boat and its smokestack to the shoebox lid. Valentines will be deposited through the smokestack and into the shoebox.

6. To make a flag, cut a 1 x 3-inch section from the remaining poster board. Fold it in half, and then open it back up. Glue a toothpick in the crease of the fold, and then glue the poster board shut.

7. Add the small heart shape stickers to both sides of the flag, and glue the flag inside one end of the boat.

8. Add fish stickers and small heart stickers to the box (the sea) and the large stickers to the boat.

9. Cut and color a small pirate from construction paper. Glue him inside the boat.

10. Glue a pipe cleaner to the pirate's arm. Tie a short piece of yarn to the opposite end of the pipe cleaner for a fishing line.

Unusual Card Slot Boxes

by
Calvin Leas

Grade 3

Hip Hoppin' Frog

Supplies

Box
Green construction paper
Glue
Scissors
Paper hole puncher
Two large rubber bands

Two large paper clips
Green poster board
Large moving eyes
Red construction paper
Black permanent marker
Green felt

Directions

1. Wrap the whole box with the green construction paper. Glue to secure.

2. Stand the box up on one end. Cut across the front about 1 inch from the top, then make two 3½-inch cuts down each front edge of the box. This will be the flap (mouth) to deposit Valentines.

3. Open the mouth and glue green construction paper onto the inside.

4. Punch two holes, one on each side of the flap (mouth). Thread a rubber band through each hole and loop tightly.

5. Glue one large paper clip inside of the box, each side of the mouth. Attach the other end of the rubber bands to the clips to allow the mouth to open and close.

6. Cut two half ovals, about 3 inches wide, from the green poster board. Glue the large moving eyes onto the half ovals, and then glue the complete eyes on the box behind the mouth flap so they stick up.

7. Cut out a large and medium heart from the red construction paper. Glue the medium heart between the eyes for the nose and the large heart under the flap on the box (body).

8. Draw a mouth on the flap with the black permanent marker.

9. Cut a 12-inch heart from the green poster board and glue it to the back of the box for the frog's back. Cut a triangle from the green poster board and glue to the bottom of the heart for legs.

10. Cut two large and two small hearts from the green felt. Glue the large hearts to the bottom corner of the triangle for hind feet. Glue the small hearts to the bottom of the box for front feet.

Unusual Card Slot Boxes

46

Valentine Monster

Supplies

Hinged shoebox
Tacky glue
Red shredded paper
Four plastic cups
Scissors

Red construction paper
Purple construction paper
Black permanent marker
White construction paper

by
Fritz Jaeger

Grade 2

Directions

1. Glue red shredded paper around the sides and top of the hinged shoebox.

2. Glue plastic cups to the bottom of the shoebox for legs.

3. Cut four large hearts from the red construction paper and glue to the plastic cups for feet.

4. Cut two medium hearts from the purple construction paper for eyes. Draw pupils on each eye with the black permanent marker. Bend at the tip and glue the tip to the top of the shoebox so the hearts (eyes) stick up.

5. Cut small hearts from the white construction paper and glue around the shoebox opening for teeth. Deposit Valentines through the "mouth."

Unusual Card Slot Boxes

47

by
**Phoebe
McLaughlin**

Grade 2

The Friendly Heart Man

 ## Supplies

Large shoebox with lid
Blue wrapping paper
Glue
Scissors

Yellow construction paper
Construction paper (assorted colors)
Black permanent marker

Directions

1. Cover the entire box with blue wrapping paper and glue to secure.

2. Cut four strips of the yellow construction paper, two as long as the shoebox and two as wide but all narrower than the sides. Glue a strip to each side of the shoebox so the ends match at the corners.

3. Cut at least 20 hearts from the construction paper (assorted colors) and glue them onto the yellow strips, six on each long side and four on each short.

4. Write in the hearts on both long sides, "Hi … Be My Valentine Sweetie," one word per heart. Make a message for the short sides as well.

5. Cut enough hearts from yellow construction paper to make a heart man—one for the head, one for the body, one for legs, and four for hands and feet. Glue them to the top of the box.

6. Cut a smiling mouth slot through the heart head and shoebox lid to deposit Valentines.

7. Draw eyes on the head with the black permanent marker. Also make "paw" lines on the hands and feet.

The Ark

Supplies

Construction paper (assorted colors)
Scissors

Pinking shears
Glue

by
Jaime Liljegren
Grade 3

Directions

1. Cut a heart from construction paper approximately 10 inches in diameter. This will be the bottom of the "box."

2. Cut smaller assorted sized hearts from construction paper using both the scissors and pinking shears.

3. Glue as many of these hearts as needed to the large heart (bottom) to form the sides of the box. Glue more hearts onto these hearts until the sides are as tall as you want them.

4. Create animals from the smaller hearts and glue around the sides to form the top of the box. Glue more animals onto these, leaving one unattached as a flap to deposit Valentines.

Unusual Card Slot Boxes

by
Tia Stanley

Grade 2

Slot Machine

 **Supplies**

Large shoebox with lid
Scissors
Empty oatmeal container
Glue
Empty small/individual cereal box
Paper towel tube

Aluminum foil
Red construction paper
White paper
Black pen
Toilet paper tube
Red cellophane wrap

Directions

1. Take the lid off the shoebox and set aside.

2. Stand the shoebox up on one of its sides. With the scissors, cut out a rectangle in the shoebox bottom, toward the bottom, as long as the oatmeal container and about 2 inches high. Cut out a square a couple inches above the rectangle, to the left, the width of the cereal box. Cut out a circle in the center of the left side of the shoebox.

3. Cut the oatmeal container in half lengthwise and slide one half into the rectangular opening, empty side up. Glue to secure.

4. Cut the individual cereal box in half lengthwise and slide one half into the square opening, empty side up. Glue to secure. Valentine cards will be deposited here and will drop into the oatmeal container (money tray).

5. Cover the entire machine with aluminum foil, wrapping the shoebox lid separately. Place the lid back on the shoebox for the back.

6. Cover the paper towel tube with red cellophane wrap and glue to secure. Wrap aluminum foil down 2 inches on one end of the tube, over the cellophane wrap.

7. Bend the paper towel tube at the aluminum foil and glue that end of the tube into the circle in the left side of the shoebox for the slot machine's handle.

8. Cut out three hearts from the red construction paper and glue them on a white rectangular piece of paper with a thin black line drawn between each heart. Glue the paper to the top front of the slot machine, with the hearts facing out.

9. Cut the toilet paper tube in half. Discard one half and cover the other half with red cellophane wrap. Glue to secure, then glue it upright to the top of the slot machine.

Unusual Card Slot Boxes

Sliding Valentines

by
Taleen Woodward

Grade 5

  ## Supplies

Scissors
Cardboard box
Construction paper (assorted
    colors)
Glue

Two white heart-shaped doilies
Red pencil
Cardboard
Black permanent marker

Directions

1. Cut the top flaps off the cardboard box.

2. Cover each side of the box with different colored pieces of construction paper, and glue to secure.

3. Glue the two heart-shaped doilies to the box, on opposite sides of the box. With the red pencil, draw and color red hearts in the center of each doily.

4. Cut hearts and assorted shapes from the construction paper and glue onto the sides of the box without a doily.

5. Cut a piece of cardboard the same width as the box but 8 inches taller. Fit it on the inside back of the box and glue to secure.

6. Cut another piece of cardboard as wide as the box and long enough to go from the top of the first piece of cardboard to the opposite side of the box. Cover it with construction paper and glue to secure.

7. Cut a large rectangular opening in the center of the cardboard to deposit Valentines. Glue one end of the cardboard to the first piece of cardboard and the other end to the opposite side of the box to form the slide.

8. Bend a piece of construction paper to form a chute and write "Drop card here" on it with the black permanent marker. Glue it above the opening in the slide.

Unusual Card Slot Boxes

51

by
Risa Royal

Grade 5

Spider—The Love Bug

  **Supplies**

Shoebox with lid
Red construction paper
Tape
Scissors
Blue construction paper
Pencil
Ruler
Black permanent marker

Glue
White construction paper
Four red pipe cleaners
Four white pipe cleaners
Large red pom-pom
Medium white pom-pom
Small pom-pom
Moving eyes

Directions

1. Wrap the shoebox, top and bottom separately, with the red construction paper. Tape to secure.

2. Cut a slot in the shoebox lid to deposit Valentines.

3. Trim the edge of the shoebox lid with the blue construction paper. Tape to secure.

4. With the pencil, trace around the ruler twice onto another piece of blue construction paper. Cut out the shapes. With the black permanent marker, write "Put Valentine here" on each strip.

5. Bend one end of each strip. Glue one bent end to the shoebox lid 2 inches to the left of the slot, and the other 2 inches to the right of the slot.

6. Cut a heart from the red construction paper wide enough to reach both strips of blue construction paper. Glue one side of the heart to one strip and the other side to the other strip.

7. Cut out two arrows from the white construction paper and glue them to the tops of the blue strips, aiming both towards the slot.

9. Bend the red and white pipe cleaners (eight total) into spider legs and glue to the bottom of the large red pom-pom (spider body), four on each side.

10. Glue the white pom-pom to the front of the body to make the spider face. Glue the moving eyes and small pom-pom (nose) to the spider face.

11. Glue the spider, standing on its legs, to the lid of the box in front of the slot.

Unusual Card Slot Boxes

Valentines, Stars & Hearts, Oh My!

by
Wenzel Stoebe
Grade 5

Supplies

Empty oatmeal container with lid.
Red construction paper
Glue
Scissors
Pencil

Pink construction paper
Black permanent marker
White construction paper
Red permanent marker

Directions

1. Wrap the oatmeal container with red construction paper, and glue to secure.

2. With the scissors, cut a star design into the lid, wide enough from point to point to deposit Valentines.

3. With the pencil, trace the lid and star design onto the pink construction paper, then cut out. Glue the pink "lid" to the red lid matching up the stars.

4. Use your black permanent marker to write the following on the lid: "Drop card in one of the slots and beat it."

5. Cut a strip of paper approximately 1 inch wide out of the pink construction paper. Glue it around the center of the oatmeal container.

6. Use the red permanent marker to draw tiny hearts around the strip of pink paper.

7. Cut out hearts from the white construction paper and glue randomly onto the container.

8. Cut out pink and red hearts slightly smaller than the white hearts. Glue these on top of the white hearts only under the strip.

Unusual Card Slot Boxes

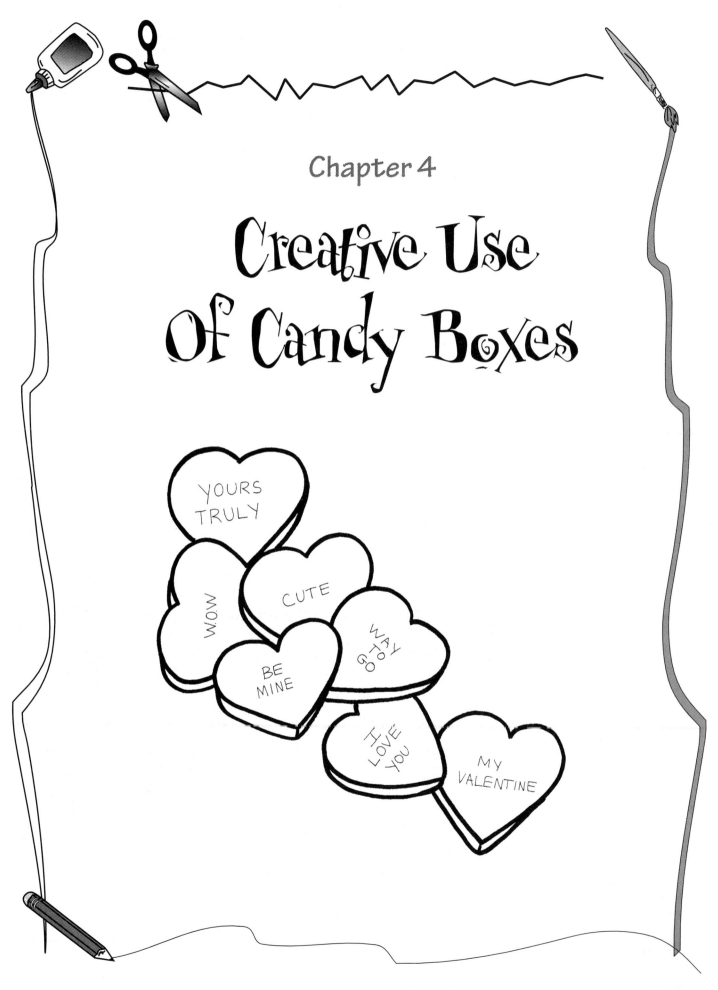

Chapter 4

Creative Use Of Candy Boxes

by
Dylan Buglewicz

Grade 1

The Candy Company NECCO just had its 150th anniversary and introduced a new computer disk candy. Printed on the candy are all kinds of computer sayings. Definitely a candy for the new Millennium.

Gingerbread Valentine House

Supplies

Glue gun
Box of graham crackers
Cardboard box with flaps
Tape
Scissors
Round disc candy
Favorite assorted candy
Four miniature Tootsie Rolls®
  (unwrapped)

Miniature marshmallows
Fruit Roll-Ups®
Toothpicks
Small heart-shaped candy
Small round candy
Kit Kat® bar
ALPHA-BITS® cereal

Directions

1. Glue graham crackers to the cardboard box, covering all the sides.

2. Bring the top flaps almost together (like the top of the house) and tape. Leave a slot at the top to deposit Valentines.

3. Glue graham crackers to the top of the box.

4. Glue the round disc candy onto the graham crackers on the roof for shingles/tiles.

5. Fill all the empty spaces with your favorite candy and glue to secure.

6. Glue four Tootsie Rolls® together for a chimney. Glue on top of the roof. Glue miniature marshmallows to the top of the chimney for smoke.

7. Cut two window panes out of the Fruit Roll-Ups® and glue to the front of the house.

8. Take six toothpicks and glue one small candy heart on each. Stick the other end of the toothpicks in miniature marshmallows and glue three to each window bottom for a shadow box.

9. Glue small round candy around the rest of the window for a frame.

10. Glue a Kit Kat® bar (three pieces) between the windows for a door. Glue two small candy hearts on the door for windows and another heart on the door for the doorknob.

11. Using ALPHA-BITS® cereal, spell "Happy Valentine's Day," and glue to the shingles/tiles on the roof.

Pick a Lollipop, Pick a Slot

by
Sydni Robson
Grade 2

Supplies

Styrofoam® heart
12-inch stick
Red spray paint
Medium square box
White spray paint
Glue
Tape
Scissors
Crayons

Five small Valentine heart stickers
Valentine lollipops (one per child in
    class)
Red permanent marker
Pink and red curling ribbon
Construction paper (Valentine
    colors)
Two red lip stickers
Two Cupid cut-outs

Directions

1. Spray paint the Styrofoam® heart and 12-inch stick with red spray paint. Let dry.
2. Spray paint the entire box white and let dry.
3. Glue the Styrofoam® heart to one end of the stick.
4. Tape the other end of the stick to the box.
5. Cut three slots in the top of the box, each big enough to deposit Valentines.
6. Draw around each slot using a different color crayon, then write the name of each color under the slot. Add a Valentine heart sticker above the slot.
7. Randomly color each lollipop stick to match one of the colors around the slots.
8. Stick the lollipops in the Styrofoam® heart. *Note:* Each child will pick a lollipop then deposit his or her Valentine in the slot that matches the color of the lollipop stick.
9. Use the red permanent marker to write the directions (see illustration below) on top of the box.
10. Tie pieces of pink and red curling ribbon to the top of the 12-inch stick and curl the ends with the scissors.

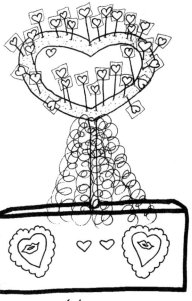

11. Cut out different size hearts from the construction paper. Glue two larger ones to the front of the box and put a red lip sticker in the center of each.
12. Decorate the rest of the box, top and sides, with the last two hearts, and both Cupid cut-outs.

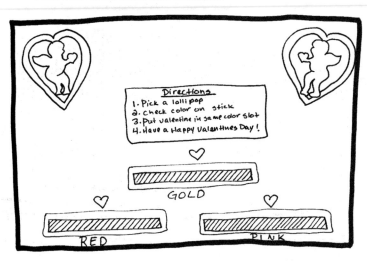

Candy Boxes

57

by
Cindy Bastron

Grade 4

Smack!

Supplies

X-acto® knife
Wooden cigar box
Glue
Red string licorice

Red hot candy
Drill
Six heart lollipops

Directions

1. Using the X-acto® knife, carefully cut a heart out of the cigar box lid, big enough to deposit Valentines.

2. Glue red string licorice in heart-shapes on the box lid.

3. Using the red-hot candy, spell out the word "SMACK" and glue it to the front side of the cigar box, leaving room on the right to shape and glue lips with the licorice.

4. Glue red-hot candy inside the licorice lips.

5. Drill six small holes around the heart slot in the lid. Stick lollipops in the holes.

Candy Boxes

Be My Sweetheart

Supplies

Scissors
White poster board
Red poster board
Glue
White correction fluid
One large conversation candy heart

Ten small boxes conversation candy
   hearts
Pencil
Two pieces red licorice

by
Michelle Ripple
Grade 4

Directions

1. Cut the white poster board in half. Cut a large heart out of one piece and a slightly smaller heart out of the red poster board.

2. Glue the red heart onto the white heart, and then cut a heart opening/slot in the middle to deposit Valentines. This will be the top of the box.

3. Using the white correction fluid, write "Be My Sweetheart" and "Net Wt. 30 Valentines" on the top of the box.

4. Glue a large candy heart to the top, and set the top aside.

5. Glue the ten candy boxes together, side by side, to make a large heart. Make sure it's smaller than the top of the box.

6. Lay the candy boxes (heart) on top of the other piece of white poster board and trace around it with the pencil.

7. Cut out the traced heart and glue it to the bottom of the candy boxes (heart).

8. Glue the top of the box to the top of the candy boxes (heart).

9. Glue one piece of red licorice sticking out from under the top, left side of the box.

10. Glue the other piece of licorice sticking out from under the top, right side of the box, opposite from the first piece of licorice to form an arrow.

11. Cut out a small triangle from the white poster board and glue it to the tip of the licorice on the right side for the arrowhead.

Candy Boxes

59

by
Erica Schumacher
Grade 4

Shiny Bear Candy Box

Supplies

Tape
Cardboard box (approx. 1 cubic ft.)
Shiny red wrapping paper
Scissors
Small teddy bear (approx. 6 inches
    tall)
Large needle
Strong thread

Velcro® (with adhesive backing)
Small red bucket
Assorted Valentine candy
Conversation candy hearts
Curling ribbon (red, gold, & silver)
Large Valentine sticker (reusable
    window artwork)
Hershey's Kisses®

Directions

1. Tape the cardboard box closed.

2. Cover the entire box with the shiny red wrapping paper and tape to secure. Cut a large heart in the top of the box to deposit Valentines.

3. Position the teddy bear in a sitting position in one corner of the top of the box. Using the large needle and strong thread, sew a couple stitches through the bear's right back leg and the top of the box, then knot the thread. Repeat for the left leg.

4. Cut the Velcro® to fit the bottom of the bucket. Stick one side to bottom of the bucket and one side to the top of the box next to the bear. Stick the bucket to the top of the box with the Velcro®.

5. Pour assorted Valentine candies into the bucket.

6. Tie pieces of curling ribbon to the bucket's handle and curl with the scissors

7. Glue the large Valentine sticker to the center front of the box.

8. Glue conversation candy hearts around the front edges of the box.

9. Glue Hershey's Kisses® and conversation candy hearts to the top and sides of the box.

Candy Boxes

Candy Heaven Box

Supplies

Scissors
Cardboard
Conversation candy hearts

Assorted candy
Large gumballs
Black permanent marker

by
Laura Airey

Grade 4

Directions

1. Cut two large hearts from the cardboard with the scissors.

2. Stack and glue conversation candy hearts around the edge of one of the hearts as high as you want the box to be. These are the sides. Put this part of the box aside.

3. Glue assorted candy on top of the other cardboard heart (box lid), placing some of the large gumballs in the center to create a handle for the box. Place this lid on the box bottom from step #2. Using the black permanent marker, write " I ❤Ya" on the top of the box.

4. Valentines are deposited by lifting the lid off the box.

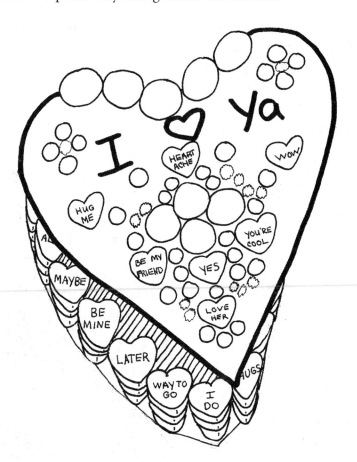

Candy Boxes

by
**Forrest
Shawn-Lee Martin**

Grade K

The Castle of Sweet Love

Supplies

Tape
Large cardboard box
Pencil
Scissors
Glue
Red wrapping paper
One small conversation candy heart

Four bags of large conversation
    candy hearts
Four tubes of pink frosting
Four toilet paper tubes
Empty oatmeal container
String

Directions

1. Tape the large cardboard box closed.

2. On the bottom center front of the box, draw the shape of a drawbridge with the pencil. Make it big enough for Valentines to enter the castle.

3. With the scissors, cut out the top and both sides of the drawbridge. Leave the bottom intact for the hinge.

4. Glue red wrapping paper to the drawbridge (in the "up" position) and then the small conversation candy heart in the middle for a handle. Open the drawbridge to deposit Valentines.

5. Glue the large conversation candy hearts, side-by-side, on all sides of the box (castle).

6. Squeeze pink frosting between the candy hearts to look like mortar.

7. Glue red wrapping paper to the top of the cardboard box.

8. Wrap the toilet paper tubes and the oatmeal container with red wrapping paper. Tape to secure.

9. Glue the oatmeal container upright onto the center top of the box, then the four toilet paper tubes upright onto the corners.

10. Cut out lots of small and medium hearts from the red wrapping paper. Glue the medium hearts, side-by-side, around the top of the oatmeal container. Glue the small hearts around the tops of the toilet paper tubes (towers).

11. Cut out four thin strips of red wrapping paper for walkways between the towers, then glue them in place.

12. Make two tiny holes, one on the left side of the drawbridge and one on the box.

13. Lace a piece of string through the holes to connect them for chains.

Candy Boxes

62

Marshmallow People

 **Supplies**

Red spray paint
Shoebox with lid (boot size)
Scissors
Glue
Red licorice pieces

Marshmallow hearts
Three Valentine heart suckers
Toothpicks
Gold glitter
Optional: Pretzel sticks

by
A. J. Haschke

Grade 3

Directions

1. Spray paint the entire shoebox red and let dry.

2. Cut a large three-sided opening in the front left corner of the lid to make a handle. The fourth side is a hinge. Cut a smaller opening in the flap formed to finish the handle. To deposit Valentines, open the shoebox lid using the handle.

3. Glue licorice pieces around the edges of the shoebox lid.

4. Glue three marshmallow hearts to the front left side of the shoebox, under the handle.

5. Create a marshmallow person by first sticking a Valentine heart sucker (head) into the top of a marshmallow heart (body). To form legs, stick a toothpick into the bottom of the marshmallow heart and attach two licorice pieces onto it, pressing them together until they stick to each other. Make the arms by sticking a toothpick into each side of the marshmallow heart and putting a licorice piece on the end. Pull off small pieces of another marshmallow and shape them into eyes, eyebrows, a nose, and a mouth. Stick them onto the sucker to form a face.

6. Repeat step #5 two more times and then glue the people lying on the shoebox lid.

7. Using glue, decorate the shoebox sides and lid with marshmallow hearts sprinkled with gold glitter.

Optional: Use pretzel sticks instead of toothpicks.

Candy Boxes

by
Nick Wolf

Grade 3

Read-A-Heart

 ## Supplies

Shoebox with lid
Red wrapping paper
Tape
Scissors

Glue
Conversation candy hearts
Conversation candy heart sticker

Directions

1. Wrap the shoebox, top and bottom separately, with the red wrapping paper. Tape to secure.

2. Cut a slot in the shoebox lid to deposit Valentines.

3. Glue the conversation candy hearts around the slot.

4. Decorate the box with lots of conversation candy heart stickers.

Candy Boxes

Candy House

by
Britney Maynard
Grade 2

Supplies

Scissors
Large white box with flaps
Glue
Red permanent marker
Valentine fabric
Red glitter

Colored pencils
Miniature marshmallows
Small conversation candy hearts
Large conversation candy hearts
Assorted candies
Red candy hearts

Directions

1. Cut the top corners off the two side flaps of the box to form triangles. Glue the front and back flaps to the side flaps, forming a roof yet leaving a large opening to deposit Valentines.

2. On both the long sides of the box (house) write "Happy Valentine's Day" with the red permanent marker.

3. Cut two hearts from the Valentine fabric and glue one on each side of the box, next to each saying above.

4. On one of the short sides of the box, draw a heart and fill it with glue then red glitter on top.

5. With the colored pencils, draw a door, grass, and bushes on the last short side of the box. This is the front of the house.

6. Alternately glue rows of miniature marshmallows and small conversation hearts on the front of the house from just above the door to the roof.

7. Glue the large conversation candy hearts and assorted candies, side-by-side, onto the front and back of the roof, then red candy hearts onto the triangle sides of the roof.

Candy Boxes

Chapter 5

Recycled Boxes

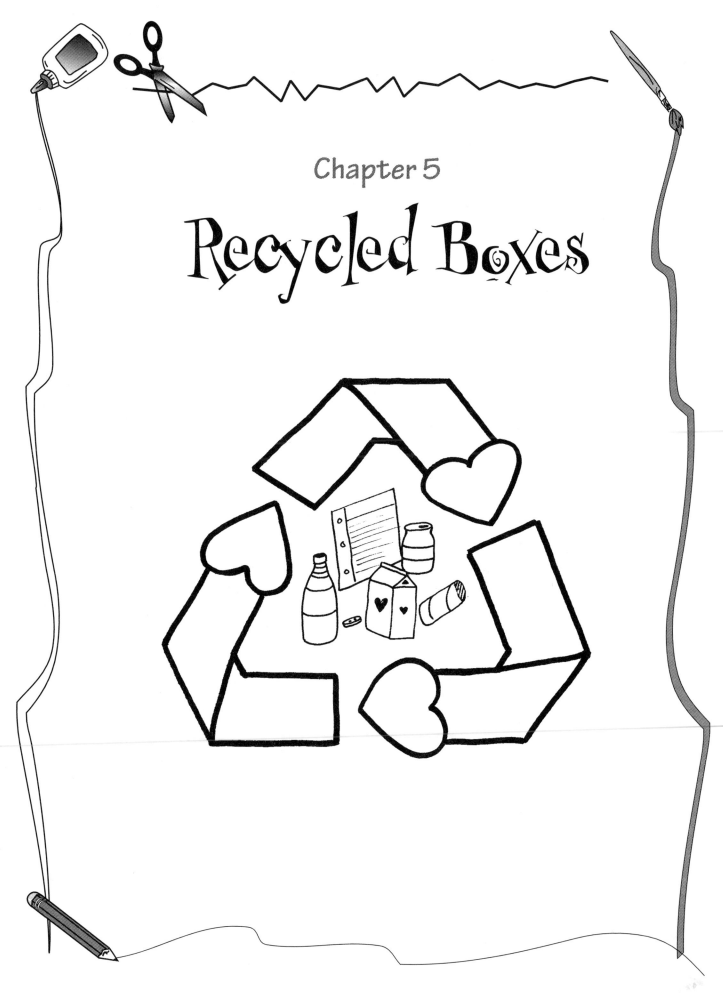

by
Jaclyn Hodson

Grade 3

Valentine's Big Smile

✂ ✏ 🖊 Supplies 🖊 ✏ ✂

Peach spray paint
One gallon empty plastic milk bottle
Paper egg carton
Scissors
White paint
Paint brushes
Blue paint
Black paint

Glue gun
Black construction paper
Pencil
Brown yarn
Empty cereal box
Red spray paint
Computer
Assorted stickers

Directions

1. Spray paint the milk bottle with the peach spray paint. Let dry.

2. Cut out two of the egg carton cups for eyes.

3. Paint the outer surface of the two egg carton cups with white paint.

4. Paint blue eyes in the center of the white painted surface, then black pupils inside the blue.

5. Glue one eye on each side of the milk bottle's handle, which will serve as the nose.

6. Cut two narrow strips of the black construction paper for eyelashes. Make sure they are long enough to go around the top half of the egg carton eyes. Cut slits in the strips to make lashes, without cutting all the way through. Curl by rolling on a pencil. Attach to the eyes with glue.

7. Loop pieces of brown yarn to make hair and attach to the head with the glue gun. Don't forget to make bangs!

8. Cut a big smile in the milk bottle under the handle (nose) to deposit Valentines.

9. Spray paint the cereal box red and let dry. Lay on its side.

10. Glue the smiling head to the cereal box.

11. On the computer, print out the words "Happy Valentine's Day!" Trim and glue to the front of the box.

12. Decorate the top of the box with stickers, around the smiling head.

"Al" the Gator

Supplies

Scissors
One gallon empty plastic milk bottle
Green construction paper

Glue
Yellow golf ball
Black felt

by
Dennis Selph

Grade 2

Directions

1. Cut a hole across the top of the milk bottle for the mouth. This is where you will deposit Valentines.

2. Cut up the green construction paper into small, odd sizes. Glue them overlapping all over the entire milk bottle.

3. Cut the yellow golf ball in half and glue one half on each side of the nose, the milk bottle's handle, for the eyeballs.

4. Cut out two small circles from the black felt. Glue one to the center of each eyeball.

5. Use green construction paper to make a tail for "Al" to sit on. Glue to the bottom of the milk bottle, sticking out.

Did you know?
A contest was held on Earth Day in 1970 for a paper-recycling symbol. There were over a thousand entries. The winning one was changed into the symbol used today, chasing arrows.

Recycled Boxes

by
Dominick Gamba

Grade 1

King of Hearts' Castle

Supplies

Four Styrofoam® packing corners
Large box with lid
Glue
Four aluminum cans
Scissors
Gift box
Stapler
Large piece packing Styrofoam®
Water bottle

Five craft sticks
Gold spray paint
Red felt
Small red Valentine stickers
Four red plastic heart jewels
Acrylic paint
Paint brushes
Plastic red heart

Directions

1. Glue the Styrofoam® packing corners onto the top corners of the large box with the lid on.

2. Glue the aluminum cans on top of the Styrofoam® corners.

3. Cut the gift box into four 8-inch half circles and one 10 ½-inch half circle. Bend to form into cones, and staple to hold. Glue the 8-inch cones on top of the cans.

4. Glue the large piece of packing Styrofoam® to the top of the box.

5. Glue the water bottle in the center of the Styrofoam® piece.

6. Glue the 10 ½-inch large cone onto the water bottle.

7. Glue craft sticks to the tips of all five cones.

8. Spray paint the whole castle with gold spray paint, about three thin even coats. Let dry thoroughly between coats.

9. Cut a slot in the top of the box between two cans and in front of the Styrofoam® piece to deposit Valentines.

10. Use some of the red felt to cut four triangular flags. Glue one flag to each craft stick on top of the cans.

11. Cut two rectangular flags from the red felt, cutting a triangle in one end of each. Hang and glue from the Styrofoam® piece, one on each side.

12. Add red heart stickers to the sides of the box.

13. Glue plastic heart jewels to the aluminum cans.

14. Decorate the large cone with paint.

15. Glue the plastic red heart to the craft stick on top of the water bottle.

Cupid's Castle

Supplies

24 toilet paper tubes
Paint brushes
Red acrylic paint
Gold acrylic paint
Large flat piece of cardboard
Glue gun
Scissors
Two empty Capri Sun® juice drink
    cartons
Empty cracker box
Empty cocoa container
    with plastic lid
Empty vanilla extract bottle

Empty ear wax remover solution
    bottle
Empty tiny bottle
Empty sunscreen bottle
Empty hairspray bottle
Pink spray paint
Toothbrush holders
Tops of squirt bottles
Deodorant dispenser tops
Plastic rings for holding pop cans
    together
Egg cartons (cut into pieces)
Bag ties

by
Kirsten Wright

Grade 4

Directions

1. Paint the 24 toilet paper tubes red, then paint the very tops of them gold, and let dry.

2. Glue the toilet paper tubes around the top edges of the cardboard and set aside.

3. Put large slots in the middle of the Capri Sun® cartons, the cracker box, and the cocoa container lid. When stacked on top of each other, Valentines will be deposited through the cocoa container and drop down through the cracker box, then both Capri Sun® cartons.

4. Glue the Capri Sun® cartons together so the slots match.

5. Glue the cracker box on top of the Capri Sun® cartons so the slots match.

6. Glue the cocoa container on top of the cracker box so the slots all line up.

7. Glue the various empty bottles onto the cracker box around the cocoa container.

8. Spray paint these boxes and bottles pink and let dry. Then glue it all onto the flat piece of cardboard inside the square of toilet paper tubes.

9. Use your imagination to decorate the box with items such as toothbrush holders, squirt bottle tops, deodorant dispenser tops, plastic rings for holding pop cans together, egg carton pieces, and bag ties.

Recycled Boxes

Years of Valentine Love

by
Thomas McNutt

Grade 1

Supplies

Glue gun
Lots of old Valentines
Heart-shaped doily

Scissors
Paper plate

Directions

1. Glue old Valentines together to make two large rectangles, approximately 12 x 16 inches.

2. Glue the long sides of the two rectangles together at the top.

3. Bend the rectangles, bringing the other long sides together, to form a tube in the shape of a heart. Glue to secure. The heart will be limp until you glue a front and back to it.

3. Make two squares out of old Valentines for the front and back of the Valentine box. In the middle of the front, glue the heart-shaped doily, then cut a heart-shaped opening in the middle to deposit Valentines.

4. Cut both the front and back into heart shapes, then glue one heart to one end of the heart tube and the other to the other end.

5. Glue your finished Valentine box to a paper plate, then cover any of the plate that is showing with more Valentines.

Valentine ♥'s Cereal

 ## Supplies

Red spray paint
Empty cereal box
Scissors

Pink construction paper
Glue
Black permanent marker

by
Kevin Hurd
Grade 3

Directions

1. Spray paint the cereal box with the red spray paint.

2. Cut out different sized hearts from the pink construction paper, and glue most to the front and one or two to each side of the box.

3. Write various Valentine messages on the hearts, such as "100% Friendship Grain" or "Low Fat." On a large heart, write the name of the cereal, "Valentine ♥'s."

4. Glue a large heart to the center back of the box. Using the black permanent marker, write "Made with 100% Goodness."

5. List the following on one side of the cereal box:

   Nutrition Facts
   - Calories—0
   - Good Feelings—100%
   - Serving Size—1 Valentine

6. Write "Net Weight 30 Valentines" on the bottom front of the box.

Recycled Boxes

73

by
Nicole Martens
Grade 5

Hearts Galore

Supplies

Empty oatmeal container with lid
(3 lb. size)
Valentine heart wrapping paper
Glue gun
Scissors
Cornmeal container lid

Two small round plastic lids
Magazines
Toilet paper tube
Plastic rings for holding pop cans
together
Pop can tabs

Directions

1. Wrap the oatmeal container and lid separately with the Valentine heart wrapping paper, and glue to secure.

2. Cut a large slot down one side of the oatmeal container to deposit Valentines, and lay the container on its side.

3. Glue the cornmeal container lid to the oatmeal container on the opposite side of the slot.

4. Cut two large hearts from the small plastic lids. Cut little hearts from magazines and glue them all over both lids.

5. Glue the lids to the oatmeal container behind the slot, sticking up.

6. Wrap the toilet paper tube with the Valentine heart wrapping paper, glue to secure, then cut the tube in half. Glue the tube halves to the oatmeal container, one on each side of the slot.

7. Cut two hearts from the Valentine wrapping paper. Glue one to the inside of each toilet paper tube.

8. Cut the plastic rings into strips. Cut small hearts from the Valentine wrapping paper and glue one heart on one end of each plastic strip. Glue the other ends inside the toilet paper tube halves.

9. Glue pop can tabs onto the oatmeal container in front of the slot.

by
Gia Genitempo
Grade 3

Valentine Express

Supplies

Shoebox with lid
Scissors
Cardboard
Glue
Paper plate

Toilet paper tube
Pink spray paint
Heart stickers
Black permanent marker

Directions

1. Cut a large slot in the shoebox lid to deposit Valentines.

2. Cut one slit for a wing in each side of the shoebox (airplane). Cut one smaller slit in each side near the back for the back wings.

3. Cut a slit in the shoebox lid near the back for the tail wing.

4. Cut out two front wings, two back wings, and a tail wing from the cardboard. Glue them in their respective slots.

5. Form a cone from the paper plate and glue it to the front of the airplane for the nose.

6. Cut the toilet paper tube in half for the engines and landing gear. Glue one under each front wing, openings forward.

7. Spray paint the entire airplane pink and let dry.

8. Stick heart stickers to the sides and wings, and around the slot. Add one sticker to the tip of the nose.

9. Using a black permanent marker, draw a cockpit and two pilots on the nose of the airplane.

Recycled Boxes

75

by
Kevin Collins

Grade 4

Titanic

Supplies

Two shoeboxes with lids
Tape
Black wrapping paper
Glue
Scissors

White construction paper
Black spray paint
Orange cellophane wrap
Tiny Valentine heart stickers

Directions

1. With the lids on, tape the shoeboxes together, end to end, to make a long ship.

2. Cover the entire ship with the black wrapping paper and glue to secure everywhere except at both ends. Form the paper at the ends into points to create the bow and the stern of the ship, and leave it alone. Cut a slot in the top of the ship toward one end to deposit Valentines.

3. Take two sheets of construction paper and roll them up together to form a smokestack. Tape to secure. Repeat three more times.

4. Spray paint the top third of the smokestacks black.

5. Glue the smokestacks to the top of the ship.

6. Wrap orange cellophane wrap around the bottom two-thirds of the smokestacks.

7. Place tiny Valentine heart stickers on the sides of the ship for portholes.

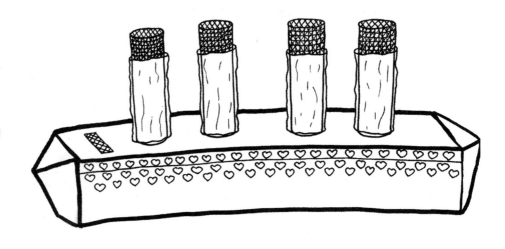

Recycled Boxes

76

Robotic Maid

  **Supplies**

by
**Andrea
Betancourt**

Grade 5

Shoebox with lid (boot-size)	Four square boxes with flaps or lids
Aluminum foil	Pencil
Tape	Pink construction paper
Scissors	Shoebox lid
Two shoeboxes with lids	Brown construction paper
Valentine wrapping paper	Black permanent marker
Glue	

Directions

1. Cover the boot-size shoebox, top and bottom separately, with the aluminum foil. Tape to secure. Put the lid on the shoebox.

2. Put the shoebox on the table, lid side down, and cut a slot in the bottom of the shoebox at one end to deposit Valentines.

3. Cover each regular shoebox and lid together with the Valentine wrapping paper. Tape to secure.

4. Glue the regular shoeboxes to each other, long sides together. Glue the short ends of the regular shoeboxes (legs) to the center of the boot-size box (feet).

5. Tape the four square boxes closed. Wrap two with the aluminum foil, and two with the Valentine wrapping paper. Tape to secure.

6. Stack the aluminum square boxes (body) on top of the legs and glue to secure.

7. Glue the Valentine paper square boxes (arms) on the body, one on each side.

8. With the pencil, draw two hands on the pink construction paper, cut them out, and glue them to the arms.

9. Wrap the shoebox lid with the Valentine wrapping paper to make the head. Tape to secure.

10. Cut out two pink hearts and glue them to the head for eyes.

11. For the hair, cut 1-inch slits about ½ inches apart (bangs) in one long side of the brown construction paper. In the opposite side of the paper, cut 4-inch slits 1 inch apart. Curl these strips by rolling them on the pencil. Glue the hair to the head with the bangs in front above the eyes and the curls in back.

12. Draw a round mouth on the head with the black permanent marker. Glue the head on top of the body.

13. Use the permanent marker to write "Happy Valentine's Day" on the front of one leg. Add two heart designs to the other leg.

Recycled Boxes

by

Tyler Sale

Grade 5

Love Lantern

Supplies

Glue
Toilet paper tube
Two foil pie pans
Wire hanger

Scissors
Blue plastic wrap
Duct tape

Directions

1. Glue the toilet paper tube upright in the center of one pie pan.

2. Shape the hanger like the filament of a light bulb (see illustration). Put the bottom of the hanger into the toilet paper tube. Glue if needed.

3. Cut a slit in the center of the second pie pan, large enough to slide the top of the hanger through. Turn the pie pan upside down and insert the top of the hanger through the slit. Pull the pie pan down over the twisted part of the hanger.

4. Cut a slot in the top of the pie pan to deposit Valentines.

5. Wrap the blue plastic wrap around the bottom pie pan up to the top pie pan. Tape both edges with duct tape to secure.

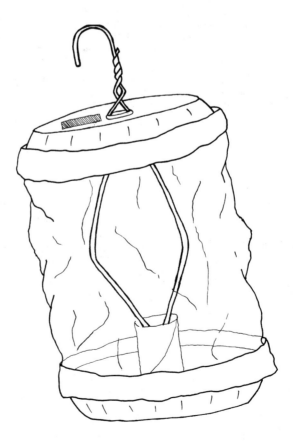

Recycled Boxes

78

Valentine Trolley

  ## Supplies

Red acrylic paint
Paint brush
Empty tissue box
Glue
Three empty pop cans

Two large marshmallows
Wagon wheel pasta
Bow tie pasta
Assorted beads

by
Kjerstin Lewis

Grade K

Directions

1. Paint the tissue box and pop cans red. Let dry.
2. Glue the pop cans on their sides to the bottom of the tissue box (trolley) for wheels.
3. Glue the two large marshmallows to the front of the trolley for headlights.
4. Glue one piece of wagon wheel pasta in the center of each pop can top and bottom (wheels).
5. Randomly glue bow tie pasta, beads, and wagon wheel pasta to the sides and top of the trolley.
6. The Valentines go into the slot on top of the tissue box.

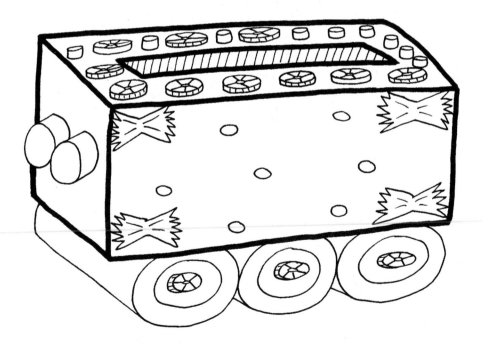

Recycled Boxes

79

Chapter 6

Easy To Make Boxes

by

Alyssa Arbuckle

Grade 2

"ABC" was a song sung by the Jackson 5, a group started in the 1970s consisting of Michael Jackson and his brothers. The chorus begins with "A-B-C, Easy as 1-2-3."

Victorian Romance

Supplies

Shoebox with lid
Shiny red wrapping paper
Glue stick
Two 6-inch heart-shaped doilies
Scissors
Four 4-inch heart-shaped doilies

Pencil
Three small packages assorted
   buttons and bows
Glue gun
Valentine stickers

Directions

1. Wrap the shoebox, top and bottom separately, with the shiny red wrapping paper. Glue to secure.

2. Place the two 6-inch doilies next to each other on top of the shoebox lid. Glue with the glue stick.

3. Cut a slot in the shoebox lid, through doilies and all, to deposit Valentines.

4. With the glue stick, glue a 4-inch doily to each side of the box, gluing it to both the lid and the shoebox. Mark where the lid meets the shoebox with the pencil, and cut so the lid can come off.

5. Arrange the buttons and bows on the shoebox and lid, and glue with the glue gun.

6. Add Valentine stickers to the sides.

Easy To Make Boxes

Lots of Hearts with Joy

  ## Supplies

by
Sabrina McCue
Grade 2

Shoebox with lid
Red heart wrapping paper
Tape
Scissors
White construction paper
Glue

Glitter
Assorted puff paints (found at craft stores)
Red bow
Red curling ribbon

Directions

1. Wrap the shoebox, top and bottom separately, with the red heart wrapping paper. Tape to secure.

2. Cut a slot in the shoebox lid to deposit Valentines.

3. Cut four small hearts from the white construction paper. Glue one heart to each corner of the lid.

4. Spread glue and then glitter around the slot.

5. Using the puff paints, draw two big hearts on the shoebox lid, one on each end of the slot.

6. Glue the red bow to the shoebox lid below the slot.

7. Tie a piece of red curling ribbon to the bow. Curl with the scissors.

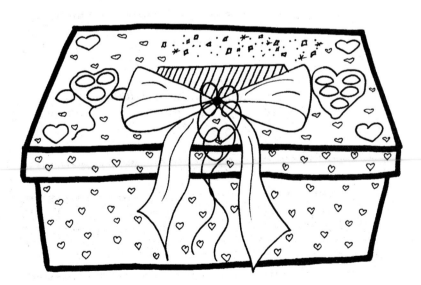

Easy To Make Boxes

83

by
Nathan Walter

Grade 1

Neighborhood Valentine Mailbox

Supplies

Scissors
Shoebox with lid
Thin piece of cardboard
Tape
Newspaper

Aluminum foil
Red poster board
Paper fastener
Valentine stickers

Directions

1. Cut a flap for the mailbox door to deposit Valentines out of one end of the shoebox.

2. Cut a piece of cardboard 2-inches wider than the lid of the shoebox. Tape it to the sides of the shoebox, with the lid on, making sure it curves over the lid. Stuff and tape newspaper between the cardboard and lid.

3. Cover the curved cardboard and shoebox (mailbox) and flap (door) with aluminum foil.

4. Make a flag from the red poster board. Attach it to the side of the mailbox with the paper fastener.

5. Decorate the mailbox with stickers.

by
Robyn Delaney

Grade 5

Shinlitter

Supplies

Shoebox with lid
Red tissue paper
Glue
Clear plastic wrap

Scissors
Heart sequins
Glitter
Curling ribbon

Directions

1. Wrap the entire shoebox (in one piece) with red tissue paper. Glue where needed, then wrap with clear plastic wrap. Glue to secure.

2. Using the scissors, cut a slot in the shoebox lid to deposit Valentines.

3. Glue heart sequins to the shoebox and lid.

4. Put glue then glitter on the lid and sides of the shoebox.

5. Glue pieces of curling ribbons to the corners of the box. Curl with scissors.

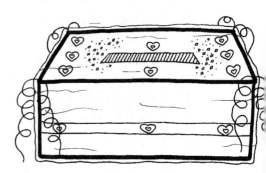

Valentine Racer

Supplies

Scissors
Shoebox with lid
White tissue paper

Glue
Stock car Valentines or car stickers
Valentine heart stickers

by
David Inbody

Grade 5

Directions

1. Wrap the shoebox, top and bottom separately, with the white tissue paper. Glue to secure.

2. Cut a slot in the shoebox lid to deposit Valentines.

3. Decorate the box with the stock car Valentines and Valentine heart stickers.

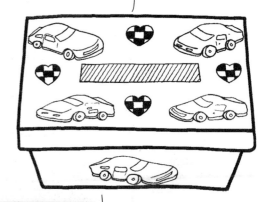

A Box of Friends

Supplies

Shoebox with lid
Red heart tissue paper
Tape

Scissors
Six Valentine heart stickers
Two pieces curling ribbon

by
Jennifer Ratterman

Grade 2

Directions

1. Wrap the shoebox, top and bottom separately, with the red heart tissue paper. Tape to secure.

2. Cut a heart shape in the lid of the shoebox to deposit Valentines.

3. Put two Valentine heart stickers on the top of the box, one next to each side of the heart shape slot. Put the remaining stickers one on each side of the box.

4. Tape a piece of ribbon next to each sticker on the top of the box only. Curl the pieces of ribbon with the scissors. Turn the box on its side.

Easy To Make Boxes

85

by

Jonathan Henricks

Grade 1

by

Alexzandria Holocker

Grade 2

Chocolate Kiss Box

Supplies

Pencil
Sand bucket
Cardboard
Scissors
Glue

Plastic grocery bag
Aluminum foil
Blue permanent marker
2-inch strip thin cardboard
Stapler

Directions

1. Trace the top of the sand bucket onto the cardboard with the pencil, and cut out the cardboard. Glue it to the top of the sand bucket.
2. Put the bucket inside the grocery bag and tie the bag closed at the top.
3. Wrap aluminum foil around the bag and bucket to look like a chocolate kiss.
4. Using the blue permanent marker, color one side of the strip of thin cardboard. Write "Happy Valentine's Day" on the other side.
5. Fold the strip of thin cardboard back and forth like an accordion. Staple it to the top of the chocolate kiss.
6. Cut a slot in front of the chocolate kiss to deposit Valentines.

Love-Notes

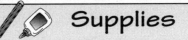

Supplies

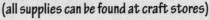

(all supplies can be found at craft stores)

Sand paper
Wooden box with lid
Tack cloth
Wooden hearts and bows
Wooden plaque

Wooden letters to spell your name
Assorted paints
Paint brushes
Glue
Varnish

Directions

1. Sand the box and use the tack cloth to remove wooden fibers.
2. Paint the wooden plaque, hearts, bows, and letters, and let them dry.
3. Glue the pieces to the box, spelling out your name on top of the plaque.
4. Using a clean paintbrush, seal the box with the varnish. Allow it to dry completely.
5. Lift the lid to deposit Valentines.

Batmobox

Supplies

Hinged shoebox
Aluminum foil
Black permanent marker

Tacky glue
Glue stick
Red glitter

by
Dayne Bieghler

Grade 5

Directions

1. Cover the hinged shoebox with aluminum foil, making sure the lid can still open to deposit Valentines.

2. Using the black permanent marker, draw two wheels on each side of the shoebox.

3. Draw a bat shape on the top of the box with tacky glue, and then sprinkle with red glitter. Let dry.

4. Rub glue from the glue stick all over the sides of the box, and then sprinkle with red glitter.

Spray, Stick & Glue

Supplies

Gold spray paint
Heart-shaped box with lid
Scissors

Glue
Doilies
Assorted stickers

by
Caroline Schafer

Grade 1

Directions

1. Spray paint the heart-shaped box and lid gold. Let them dry thoroughly.

2. With the scissors, cut a slot in the lid to deposit Valentines.

3. Glue doilies around the slot and around the edge of the lid.

4. Add stickers to the lid and sides of the box.

5. Rub glue all over the box, doilies, and stickers, and allow it to dry thoroughly.

Easy To Make Boxes

87

Love Bug

by

Moriah VanCleef

Grade 2

Supplies

Tape
Medium box with flaps
Scissors
Light blue construction paper

Red construction paper
Pink construction paper
Pinking shears
Glue

Directions

1. Tape up the box so the flaps are closed.
2. Cover the box with light blue construction paper and tape to secure.
3. Cut a slot in the top of the box to deposit the Valentines.
4. Cut two medium-size hearts from the red construction paper and glue on the front of the box for eyes.
5. Cut one small heart from the dark blue construction paper and glue under the eyes for a nose.
6. Cut six smaller hearts from assorted colors of construction paper and shape and glue them under the nose for a mouth.
7. Cut four medium-size hearts from the pink construction paper and glue two sticking out from the box for ears.
8. Use the pinking shears to cut one 1 x 12-inch strip of paper from the dark blue construction paper and one from the red construction paper.
9. Cut two 1-inch slits in the top of the box, one on each side of the Valentine slot. Insert the strips, one in each slit, and secure with glue.
10. Glue the remaining two pink hearts to the ends of the strips, one heart per strip.

Easy To Make Boxes

88

Special Delivery

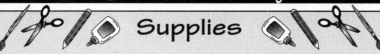

Supplies

Shoebox with lid	Red permanent marker
Red construction paper	Foil-covered chocolate heart
Glue	Cardboard
Scissors	Paper fastener
White poster board	

Directions

1. Wrap the shoebox, top and bottom separately, with the red construction paper. Glue to secure.
2. Cut a slot in the shoebox lid to deposit Valentines.
3. Cut two pieces from the white poster board as wide as the ends of the shoebox, but higher and curved on the top like the door of a mailbox. Glue one piece on each end of the shoebox, flat side flush with the bottom of the shoebox.
4. Using the red permanent marker, write the word "MAIL" on one of the curved pieces and "BOX" on the other.
5. Glue the foil-covered chocolate heart under the word "MAIL."
6. Cut a mailbox flag from the cardboard and color with the red permanent marker.
7. Attach the flag to one side of the shoebox (mailbox) with the paper fastener.

Ryan

by

Miller

rade K

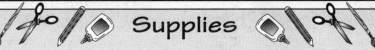

Valentine Mailbox on a Stand

Supplies

Shoebox with lid
Valentine heart wrapping paper
Tape
X-acto® knife
Scissors

Pink cord or rope
Pink construction paper
Red glitter glue
Red permanent marker
Four small wooden blocks

Directions

1. Wrap the shoebox, top and bottom separately, with the Valentine wrapping paper. Tape to secure.

2. Stand the shoebox on one short side, bottom of the box facing you. Use the X-acto® knife to cut a three-sided mailbox slot near the top of the shoebox. Leave the bottom side of the slot intact for a hinge.

3. Poke two holes in the flap formed. Thread the pink cord through the holes and knot on the inside of the flap for a handle. Pull the handle to deposit Valentines.

4. Cut out the letters "V-A-L-E-N-T-I-N-E-M-A-I-L" from the pink construction paper. Cover the letters with red glitter glue and let dry.

5. Glue the letters onto the box under the flap, so they spell out VALENTINE MAIL.

6. Use the red permanent marker to make a sign on the pink construction paper that says, "Pickup Time: February 14th." Glue it above the mail slot.

7. Glue the four wooden blocks to the bottom of the mailbox to make legs, making sure to leave room to put the lid back on the shoebox.

Double-Decker Valentine Box on Wheels

by
Samantha Post

Grade 5

...lies

Scissors
Two shoeboxes (one with lid)
Paints (assorted colors)
Paintbrushes

Glue
Rope or cord
Four wooden wheels and screws

Directions

1. Cut a slot in the shoebox lid to deposit Valentines.
2. Cut a slot in either side of the other shoebox, also to deposit Valentines. (Children can decide which slot they want to use.)
3. Decorate the boxes with paint however you want, and let them dry.
4. Glue the shoebox with lid on top of the open shoebox.
5. Punch a hole in the bottom box on one end. Thread the rope through the hole and knot on the inside.
6. Screw the wheels into the corners of the bottom box, on the long sides so the double-decker Valentine box will roll when pulled by the rope.

Note: Valentines can also be deposited into the open shoebox.

Easy To Make Boxes

by

Raeanne Johnson

Grade 3

Cupid's Heart Box

Supplies

Large round cardboard container
    with lid
White paper
Tape
Pink plastic wrap
Scissors
Red stick-on letters
Glue

Heart-decorated ribbon (to go
    around the top and bottom of
    the container)
Cupid, heart, and lip stickers
    (assorted sizes)
Red twisted craft paper (found in
    craft stores)

Directions

1. Wrap the cardboard container, top and bottom separately, with the white paper. Tape to secure.

2. Rewrap the container, top and bottom separately, with the pink plastic wrap. Tape to secure.

3. Cut a slot in the lid of the cardboard container to deposit the Valentines.

4. Using the red stick-on letters, spell out your name and stick it on top of the box above the slot.

5. Glue ribbon around the top of the lid and the bottom of the container.

6. Decorate the box and lid with the Valentine stickers.

7. Using the scissors, punch a small hole on both sides of the box. Insert the red twisted craft paper into the holes to form a handle, and secure with glue.

Easy To Make Boxes

by
Jacob Keller
Grade 3

Girls' Cards / Boys' Cards

  ## Supplies

Scissors
Plain shoebox with lid
Crayons
Construction paper (assorted
    colors)

Glue
Cardboard
Black permanent marker
Optional: White wrapping paper

Directions

1. Cut two slots in the shoebox lid, one on each end, to deposit Valentines.

2. Draw hearts on the sides of the shoebox with the crayons.

3. Cut out hearts from the construction paper and glue onto the shoebox lid.

4. From the cardboard, cut out two square pieces as wide as the slots. With the black permanent marker, write "Girls' cards" on both sides of one piece and "Boys' cards" on both sides of the other. Tape one piece sticking up from one slot and the other piece from the other slot.

Optional: If you do not have a plain shoebox, wrap the shoebox and lid separately with the white wrapping paper, tape to secure, then go to step #1.

Chapter 7

Jokes, Puns
& Poem Boxes

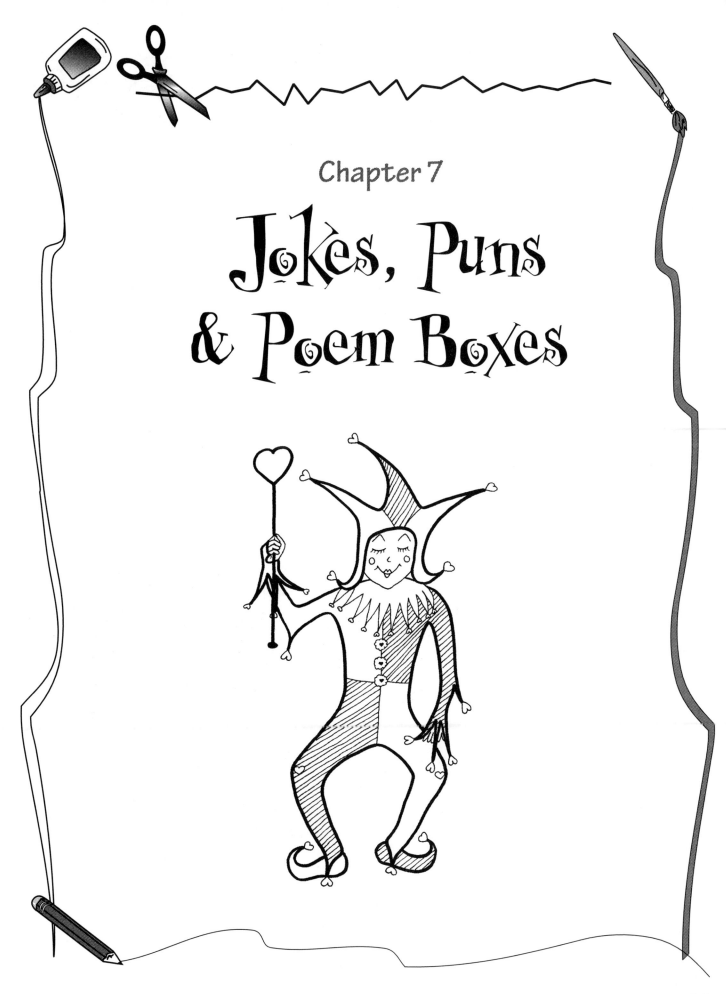

by

Schuyler Burks

Grade 4

In the 1400s, people avoided Jesters because they thought they were contagious.

Jokes, Puns & Poems

Cartoon Character Can

Supplies

Empty coffee can with lid
Red tissue paper
Glue
Scissors

White construction paper
Old Valentines
Black permanent marker
Clear Con-Tact® paper

Directions

1. Wrap the coffee can and lid separately with the red tissue paper. Glue to secure.

2. Cut heart shapes from the white construction paper and randomly glue them onto the can.

3. Cut cartoon characters from old Valentines. Glue the characters next to the hearts on the can so they appear to be communicating with each other.

4. Make up things the cartoon characters might say to each other, such as "This party was a bright idea." Write them on the hearts with the black permanent marker.

5. When you are finished decorating the can, cover it and the lid with clear Con-Tact® paper.

6. Cut a wide slot in the coffee can lid to deposit Valentines.

Lady with the Blue Face

by
Katie Markegard
Grade 3

Supplies

Blue spray paint
Styrofoam® ball
Scissors
Two empty plastic milk bottles
   (gallon size)
Glue gun
Black yarn
Red yarn
Moving eyes
Pink heart button

Red heart button
Doll hat
White paper
Crayons
¼ -yard Valentine fabric
Velcro® (with adhesive backing)
Red felt
Wooden heart
Black permanent marker
Stick

Directions

1. Spray paint the Styrofoam® ball blue and let it dry.

2. Using the scissors, cut the handle off one of the plastic milk bottles and throw away the bottle. Glue the handle onto the other milk bottle, opposite the other handle.

3. Glue the Styrofoam® ball (head) to the top of the milk bottle. Position the bottle with one handle on your left and one on your right to finish the doll.

4. Glue strands of black yarn to the head for hair and braid it. Secure the braids with pieces of red yarn tied into bows.

5. Glue the moving eyes to the head. Finish the face using the pink heart button for the nose and the red heart button for the mouth.

6. Glue the doll hat on top of the head.

7. Cut out bloomers (underwear) from the white paper and decorate them with the crayons.

8. Cut the Valentine fabric to fit like a dress around the bottle. Use Velcro® to hold the dress together.

9. Cut out hearts from the red felt for hands and glue to the outside of the dress on the handles (arms).

10. Write the following poem on your wooden heart with the black permanent marker: "I'm the lady with the blue face. My birthplace is Outerspace."

11. Glue the heart to the stick and the stick to the right arm.

12. Cut a slot in the bottle's back just above the dress to deposit Valentines.

Jokes, Puns & Poems

97

by
Mitchell Cowan

Grade 2

The Joke's on You!

Supplies

Shoebox with lid
Paper grocery bag
Glue

Scissors
Pink construction paper
Colored markers

Directions

1. Wrap the shoebox, top and bottom separately, with the paper grocery bag. Glue to secure.

2. Cut a slot in the shoebox lid to deposit Valentines.

3. Cut out different size hearts from the pink construction paper and glue all except one large one onto the sides and lid of the shoebox. It's fine if they hang over the edges.

4. Fold the remaining large heart in half and write the following joke on the outside of the heart: "What do you get from 2 banana peels?" Open up the heart to write the answer: "A double slide." Glue the heart onto the lid next to the slot.

5. Draw your own design on the rest of the box using the colored markers.

Valentine Robot

by
Martin Milius
Grade 5

 ## Supplies

Scissors
Two shoeboxes with lids
Two toilet paper tubes
Aluminum foil

Glue gun
Red construction paper
Red permanent marker
1 x 3-inch white paper

Directions

1. Cover shoeboxes (with lids on) and toilet paper tubes with the aluminum foil.

2. Stand one shoebox (body) on its end, and glue the other shoebox (head) on its side on top of it. Cut a large open mouth in the front of the head to deposit Valentines.

3. Glue the toilet paper tubes (arms) onto the body, one on each side.

4. Shape the aluminum foil into a pair of antennae, and glue them on top of the head.

5. Cut out two hearts from the red construction paper and glue one onto the end of each antenna.

6. Draw a face onto the head with the red permanent marker.

7. Cut out a large red heart and glue it to the front of the body. Draw an alien face inside the heart with the black permanent marker.

8. Write the following poem on the white paper and glue it onto the right arm:

> My robot's
> Name is Scott
> Please put your
> Valentine
> In his slot

by

Weston Markegard

Grade 1

Dragon with a Broken Heart

Supplies

1-liter empty soft drink bottle
Scissors
Green felt
Glue gun
Green craft foam
Two moving eyes
Pinking shears

Green pom-poms
Thin wire
Orange construction paper
Yellow construction paper
Red felt
Black permanent marker
Heavy cardboard

Directions

1. Rinse out the soft drink bottle and let dry. Discard the cap.

2. Cut an inch off the top of the bottle. Wrap the bottle with green felt and glue to secure.

3. Cut two dragon heads/mouths from the green craft foam. Put one on top of the other and glue them together from the middle to the one end. Glue the glued part (head) to the top of the bottle, leaving the open part (mouth) sticking out from the bottle.

4. Glue the moving eyes to the top of the head.

5. Use the pinking shears to cut a pointy tail from the green craft foam. Glue the tail onto the side of the bottle below the head and eyes (dragon's back).

6. Glue green pom-poms in a row down the tail for scales.

7. Cut two wings from the green felt and glue them on either side of the tail, pointing towards the back of the dragon.

8. Poke a hole under the tail with the wire and push it up through the dragon's mouth for the "tongue."

9. Cut orange and yellow construction paper into fire-like pieces, and glue them to the wire (tongue) inside the mouth.

10. Cut two feet from the green craft foam and glue them to the front bottom of the bottle.

11. Cut a slot in the front of the bottle (dragon's belly) to deposit Valentines.

Dragon with a Broken Heart *(cont.)*

12. Cut out a large heart from the red felt. Cut it in half and glue one half on each side of the slot.

13. Using a black permanent marker, write the following poem on the heart: "My heart will break in 2 if I don't get a Valentine from you."

14. Cut the cardboard into a stand for the dragon. Cover with green felt and glue to secure. Glue the dragon to the stand.

Jokes, Puns & Poems

Chapter 8

Bags & Envelope Boxes

by
Lance Allen

Grade 2

A bag can also mean a pouch, purse, briefcase, backpack, doggie bag, knapsack, or grip. Can you think of some other words?

The Love Envelope

Supplies

Scissors
Red poster board
Paper hole puncher

White yarn
Black permanent marker

Directions

1. With the scissors, cut two large identical hearts out of the red poster board.

2. Place the hearts directly on top of each other. Punch holes about 2 inches apart around the outer edges of the hearts, but not across the top.

3. Knot one end of the white yarn and weave the opposite end through the holes, starting at the top of one side and ending at the opposite side. Knot the end of the yarn.

4. Draw designs on the front of the envelope with the black permanent marker.

5. Valentines can be deposited into the top of the envelope.

Bags & Envelopes

Queen of Hearts' Felt Bag

 ## Supplies

by
Becky Neuman

Grade 2

Two 8 ½ x 11-inch pieces red felt

Sewing machine

Tacky glue

One 8 ½ x 11-inch piece light pink felt

Scissors

Pencil

Two red buttons

White thread and needle

1-inch piece Velcro®

Assorted pieces of felt
(Valentine colors)

Directions

1. Put the two red felt pieces together to make a bag. Glue or sew the two long sides and one short side together. Turn inside out if sewn.

2. Fold the light pink felt piece in half widthwise and glue or sew the short sides together. Turn inside out if sewn.

3. Lay this pink "flap" over the open part of the red bag with the folded side in front. Glue the raw edges of the flap to the top back of the bag.

4. Cut a large slot through both layers in the top of the flap to deposit the Valentines.

5. Measure and mark where you would like the buttons to go on the flap. Sew them in place by hand. *Note:* Be careful not to sew the flap to the box.

6. Glue or sew the Velcro® between the flap and box.

7. Cut an assortment of small, medium, and large hearts out of the assorted pieces of felt. Stack up to three different sizes together, and then glue them in place on the bag.

Bags & Envelopes

105

by
Jason Hamblen

Grade 5

Quick & Easy Valentine Envelope

Supplies

White poster board
Stapler

Permanent markers

Directions

1. Fold the poster board in half widthwise.

2. Staple the two short sides together.

3. Using the permanent markers, personalize the front of the poster board with your name.

4. Then add the word "Valentines" and draw hearts around your name.

5. Valentines can simply be dropped into the envelope.

The Love-Lee Purse

  **Supplies**

by
Casey D'Alanno

Grade 1

Pinking shears
11 x 14-inch purple construction
 paper
11 x 14-inch pink construction paper
Glue
Stapler

Three doilies
Valentine heart stickers
Black permanent marker
Red construction paper
Scissors

Directions

1. Use your pinking shears to cut out two large hearts, one from the purple construction paper and one from the pink.

2. Put glue around the edges of both hearts, except the tops, and then stick them together.

3. Staple around the edges where you have glued, leaving the top open.

4. Cut a 1 x 12-inch strip from each piece of construction paper.

5. Lay the strips together and staple one end inside the heart "purse" at one side of the top, and the other end at the other side. Now you have your handle.

6. Glue the three doilies to one side of the purse. Put one Valentine sticker in the center of each doily, and additional stickers around the doilies.

7. Draw a large heart on the opposite side of the purse with the black permanent marker. Cut hearts from the red construction paper using regular scissors and make a ladybug to glue on the purse over the large drawn-on heart. Draw heart eyes, a nose, mouth and antennae on your ladybug with your black permanent marker. Cut two additional hearts from red construction paper; glue them above the ladybug and write "I Love You" on them.

Bags & Envelopes

107

by
Julia Terrell

Grade 6

The Five Minute Valentine Bag

Supplies

Store-bought Valentine gift bag
(preferably with a big heart
design)

Stapler
Scissors
Optional: Stapler

Directions

1. Use your scissors to poke a hole into the bag, then cut around the top of the heart or Valentine design on the bag.

2. Pull the heart towards you slightly without ripping the bag. Valentines can be deposited through this opening or into the bag.

Note: It is important to find a bag with a design like a heart, which allows you to cut an opening to deposit Valentines.

Optional: Staple the top opening of the bag closed, leaving the handles on the outside.

Bags & Envelopes

Stay Awake, Make It & Take It

 ## Supplies

Scissors
Red poster board

Glue
Red gift bag

by
Whitney Buckner
Grade 4

Directions

1. Cut two very large hearts from the red poster board and glue one to the front of the gift bag and one to the back. Valentines can be dropped into the gift bag. You're ready to go—it's easy.

Bags & Envelopes

Roses are Red,
Violets are Blue,
Aren't these
Valentine Boxes,
Fun to put together
and glue?

Till next time
Willie

Thoughts

Final

110

Index

111

Order Form

Become an expert the easy way! Order from the What Do I Do?® series
CALL OUR TOLL FREE HOTLINE TO ORDER TODAY AT:

1-888-738-1733

Oakbrook Publishing House
P.O. Box 2463 • Littleton, CO 80161-2463
Phone: (303) 738-1733 • Fax: (303) 797-1995
Website: **http://www.whatdoidobooks.com** • E-mail: **Oakbrook@whatdoidobooks.com**

Mail To

Name: _____

Address: _____

City, State & Zip Code: _____ Phone:(____) _____

❥ Order 2 books and get a 10% discount or order 3 or more books and get a 10% discount and free shipping.

Book Title	Quantity	Price	Total
Halloween School Parties … What Do I Do?® ISBN: 0-9649939-8-8	_____	$19.95 ea.	$_____
Valentine School Parties … What Do I Do?® ISBN: 0-9649939-9-6	_____	$19.95 ea.	$_____
Valentine Boxes … What Do I Do?® ISBN: 0-9649939-3-7	_____	$12.95 ea.	$_____
		SUBTOTAL	$_____
		Shipping & Handling *(see below)*	$_____
		Colorado Res. Add 3.8% Sales Tax	$_____
		Discount	$_____
		TOTAL	$_____

❏ Check or Money Order payable to: Oakbrook Publishing House
❏ Credit Card: Visa ❏   Master Card ❏   Discover ❏

Card Number _____ Exp. Date _____

Signature _____

❥ Canadian orders must be accompanied by a postal money order in U.S. funds.

❥ Shipping and Handling charges are:
1st class $3.75, 4th class $2.25 (Allow 7–10 days for 4th class mail), additional books add $1.15 each.

❤ 100% fully guaranteed on all orders. ❤

COMING SOON
Slumber Parties … What Do I Do?® • *Christmas Parties … What Do I Do?*® • *Teacher's Gifts … What Do I Do?*®